Advanced Level

Six-Way paragraphs

Revised and Expanded

100 Passages for Developing the Six
Essential Categories of Comprehension

Walter Pauk, Ph.D.
Director, Reading Research Center
Cornell University

Jamestown Publishers

Six-Way Paragraphs
Advanced Level

Catalog No. 731
© 1983 by Jamestown Publishers, Inc.

Cover Design by Deborah Hulsey Christie.

Printed in the United States of America
     10 BB 97 96

ISBN: 0-89061-303-6

Readability
Passages 1–20:   Level H
Passages 21–40:   Level I
Passages 41–60:   Level J
Passages 61–80:   Level K
Passages 81–100: Level L

Preface

Learning by Doing

"Please let me do this one by myself." These words echo the age-old principle of learning by doing. And this basic "hands-on" principle works because it makes students *concentrate* and it makes them *think*.

Concentrate. First, to make students concentrate, we compiled stories about what I believe are among the world's most fascinating factual episodes and facts of nature. The stories in this revised and expanded edition of *Six-Way Paragraphs* are all new.

Think. Second, to make students think, we devised six types of questions, which are the only ones that can be legitimately asked about factual prose.

Practice. By answering these six types of questions over and over again, each time in a different context, students learn what to look for when reading factual prose. And once these skills are learned it is easy and natural to carry them over to the reading of textbooks.

In brief, by making students concentrate on factual stories and questions, this book provides a systematic and certain way for teachers to teach and learners to learn.

Acknowledgments

Although I assume complete responsibility for the faults of this book, I am happy to acknowledge my indebtedness to students and colleagues for many of its strong points. The students in all my classes have been helpful in their suggestions and enthusiasm. Graduate students, colleagues and teachers too numerous to mention individually provided criticism when I needed it most. I wish, however, to single out Walter Brownsword, former chairman of the English Department of Community College of Rhode Island, for especial thanks for refining the six-way questions in the first edition. The staff of Jamestown Publishers has been unstintingly helpful in supporting these efforts, through genuine encouragement, and design and editorial assistance in both editions. To all, I am deeply grateful.

Walter Pauk

Ithaca, New York
March 1983

Contents

Titles of Passages

The Paragraph

The paragraph! That's the working-unit of both writer and reader. The writer works hard to put meaning into the paragraph; the reader works hard to take meaning out of it. Though they work at opposite tasks, the work of each is closely related. Actually, to understand better the job of the reader, one must first understand better the job of the writer. So, let us look briefly at the writer's job.

One Main Idea. To make their meaning clear, writers know that they must follow certain basic principles. First, they know that they must develop only one main idea per paragraph. This principle is so important that they know it backward, too. They know that they must not try to develop two main ideas in the same paragraph.

The Topic Sentence. The next important principle they know is that the topic of each main idea must be stated in a topic sentence, and that such a sentence best serves its function by coming at or near the beginning of its paragraph. They know too, that the more clearly they can state the topic of a paragraph in an opening sentence, the more effective they will be in developing a meaningful, well-organized paragraph.

One word of warning to the reader: there is no guarantee that the topic sentence will always be the first sentence of a paragraph. Occasionally, a writer will start off with an introductory or a transitional sentence. Then, it is up to the reader to spot such a sentence, and recognize it for what it is.

The topic sentence may be placed in several other positions in a paragraph. It may be placed in the middle, or even at the very end. If it appears at the end, though it may still be a topic sentence in form, in terms of function, it is more rightfully a *restatement*. Whenever the end position is chosen, it is chosen to give the restatement especial emphasis.

Finally, a paragraph may not have a topic sentence in it at all. Some writers purposely leave out such sentences. But, in such cases, inferring a topic sentence may not be as difficult as it may at first appear. Here's why. Inside information has it that many such professional writers actually do write topic sentences, but on separate scraps of paper. They then place one of the scraps at the head of a sheet and use the topic sentence to guide their thoughts in the construction of the paragraph. With the paragraph written and the topic sentence having served its purpose, the scrap is discarded. The end result is a paragraph without a visible topic sentence, but the paragraph, nonetheless, has embedded in it all the clues that an alert reader needs for making an accurate inference.

Finding Meaning. Actually, there is nothing especially important in recognizing or inferring a topic sentence for its own sake. The important thing is that the reader use the topic sentence as a quick means of establishing a focal point around which to cluster the meanings of the subsequent words and sentences that he or she reads. Here's the double-edged sword again: just as writers use topic sentences to provide focus and structure for presenting their meaning, so the perceptive reader can use the topic sentence for focus and structure to gain meaning.

Up to this point, the reader, having looked secretly over the writer's shoulder, should have learned two exceedingly valuable secrets: first, to always look for only *one* main idea in each paragraph; and secondly, to use the topic sentence to discover the topic of each paragraph.

Supporting the Main Idea. Now, there is more to a writer's job than writing paragraphs that consist of only bare topic sentences and main ideas. The balance of the job deals with *developing* each main idea through the use of supporting material which amplifies and clarifies the main idea and, many times, makes it more vivid and memorable.

To support their main ideas, writers may use a variety of forms. One of the most common is the *example*. Examples help to illustrate the main idea. Other supporting materials are anecdotes, incidents, jokes, allusions, comparisons, contrasts, analogies, definitions, exceptions, logic and so forth.

To summarize, the reader should have learned from the writer that a textbook-type paragraph usually contains these three elements: a topic sentence, a main idea, and supporting material. Knowing this, the reader should use the topic sentence to find the main idea. Everything other than the main idea is supporting material used to illustrate, amplify, and qualify the main idea. So, the reader must be able to separate the main idea from the supporting material, yet see the relationship between them.

To the Instructor

The Reading Passages. Each of the 100 passages included in the book had to meet the following three criteria: *high interest level, appropriate readability level,* and *factual content.*

The high interest level was assured by choosing passages of mature content that would appeal to a wide range of readers.

The readability level of each passage was computed by applying Dr. Edward B. Fry's *Formula for Estimating Readability,* thus enabling the arrangement of passages according to grade levels within the book. *Six-Way Paragraphs, Middle Level* contains passages that range from grade 4 to grade 8 reading level, with twenty passages on each grade level. The passages in *Six-Way Paragraphs, Advanced Level* range from grade 8 to grade 12 readability, with twenty passages on each reading level.

The factual content was a definite requirement because by reading factual passages students build not only their reading skills, but, of equal importance, their informational backgrounds.

The Six Questions. This book is organized around six essential questions. And the bright jewel in this array is the exciting main idea question, which is actually a set of three statements. Students must first choose and label the statement that expresses the *main idea* of the passage, then they must label each of the other statements as being either *too narrow* or *too broad* to be the main idea.

In addition to the main idea question, there are five other questions. These questions are within the framework of the following five categories: subject matter, supporting details, conclusions, clarifying devices, and vocabulary in context.

By repeated practice with the questions within these six categories, students will develop an active, searching attitude that will carry over to the reading of other expository prose. These six types of questions will help them become aware of what they are reading at the time they are actually seeing the words and phrases on a page. This type of thinking-while-reading sets the stage for higher comprehension and better retention.

The Diagnostic Chart. This Diagnostic Chart provides the most dignified form of guidance yet devised. With this Chart, no one has to point out a student's weaknesses. The Chart does that automatically, yielding the information directly and personally to the student, making self-teaching possible. The organization of the questions and the format for marking answers on the Chart are what make it work so well.

The six questions for each passage are always in the same order. For example, the question designed to teach the skill of drawing conclusions is always the fourth question, and the main idea question is always first. This innovation of keeping the questions in a set order sets the stage for the smooth working of the Chart.

The Chart works automatically when the students write the letter of their answer choices for each passage in the spaces provided. Even after completing only one passage, the Chart will reveal the type or types of questions answered correctly, as well as the types answered incorrectly. As the answers for more passages are recorded, the Chart will show the types of questions that are missed consistently. A pattern can be seen after three or more passages have been completed. For example, if a student answers question number four (drawing conclusions) incorrectly for three out of four passages, the student's weakness in this area shows up automatically.

Once a weakness is revealed, have your students take the following steps: First, turn to the instructional pages in the beginning of the book, and study the section in which the topic is discussed. Second, go back and reread the questions that were missed in that particular category. Then, with the correct answer to a question in mind, read the entire passage again, trying to see how the author developed the answer to the question. Do this for each question that was missed. Third, when reading future passages, make an extra effort to correctly answer the questions in that particular category. Fourth, if the difficulty continues, arrange to see the teacher.

To the Student

The Six Types of Questions

In this book, the basic skills necessary for reading factual material are taught through the use of the following six types of questions: *subject matter, main idea, supporting details, conclusion, clarifying devices*, and *vocabulary in context*. Let us take a closer look at each of these types of questions.

Subject Matter. This question looks easy and is easy. But don't let that fool you into thinking it isn't important. It can teach you the most important skill of all reading and learning: concentration. With it, you comprehend and learn. Without it, you fail.

Here's the secret for gaining concentration: After reading the first few lines of something, ask yourself, "What is the subject matter of this passage?" Instantly, you will be thinking about the passage. You will be concentrating.

If you don't ask this question, your eyes will move across the lines of print, yet your mind will be thinking of other things.

By asking this question as you read each passage in this book, you will master the skill so well that it will carry over to everything you read.

Let's see how this method works. Here is a short passage:

> Do you want to be a good speaker? If so, then think *before* you speak, and think *while* you speak. Take care to pronounce words well. Do not speak your words too hastily. Use words your audience can understand. Do not speak in the same tone all the time. Cut out all mannerisms such as making the same gesture over and over again. Do not point or jab your finger at the audience. And don't forget to use your voice to express your feelings.

On finishing the first sentence, I hope you said to yourself, "Ah! a passage on speaking. Maybe I can pick up a few good tips." If you use this technique, you'll be concentrating, you'll be looking for something, your attitude will be superb, and, best of all, you'll be comprehending, learning, and remembering.

Main Idea. In reading anything, once you have grasped the subject matter, ask yourself, "What point is the writer trying to make?" Once this question is asked, your mind will be looking for an answer, and chances are that you will find one. But when no question is asked, all things seem equal. Nothing stands out.

Let's try to find the main idea by asking, "What point is the writer trying to make?" in the following passage:

> A horseshoe means good luck. This is true in every country. The good luck comes partly because the shoe is made of iron, and also because its shape is like a crescent moon. It is very good luck to find a horseshoe by the side of the road. It is extra good luck if the shoe was thrown from the right rear leg of a grey mare. Horseshoes are usually hung over the outside doorways of houses.

I think we'd all agree that a good answer is, "Horseshoes mean good luck." In this passage, we were lucky that the first sentence is an excellent *topic sentence.*

The next example does not have a topic sentence. Nevertheless, we'll ask again, "What point is the writer trying to make?" This time, however, you'll have to think about the passage and come up with your own answer.

> What will the newborn baby be like when it grows up? Friends and parents would like to know. Some people believe you can find out by placing a coin in the child's right hand. If the baby holds the coin tightly, it means that the child will grow up to save money. If it is held loosely, it means the baby will be generous. If the coin is dropped, the child will be a spender.

No doubt you had to *think* to come up with an answer. In this case, the answer had to be a summary type answer. Compare your answer with the following main idea statement: "Some people use a coin to try to find out a baby's future."

Supporting Details. In common usage, the word *detail* has taken on the unrespected meaning of "something relatively unimportant." But details are important. Details are the plaster, board and brick of a building, while main ideas are the large, strong steel or wooden beams. Both are necessary for a solid paragraph.

The bulk of a factual paragraph is made up of details that support the main idea. The main idea is often buried among the details. You have to dig to distinguish between them. Here are some characteristics that can help you see the difference between supporting details and main ideas.

First, supporting details come in various forms, such as examples, explanations, descriptions, definitions, comparisons, contrasts, exceptions, analogies, similes, and metaphors.

Second, these are used to support the main idea. The words themselves, *supporting details*, spell out their job. So, when you have trouble finding the main idea, take the paragraph apart sentence by sentence, asking, "Does this sentence support something, or is this the thing being supported?" In other words, you must not only separate the two, but also see how they help one another. The main idea can often be expressed in a single sentence. But a sentence cannot tell a complete story. The writer must use additional sentences to give you the full picture.

The following passage shows how important details are for providing a full picture of what the writer had in mind.

> This book has provided us with a marvelous record of village life in the mountains of Lebanon 100 years ago. In one picture, we see women baking bread in clay ovens, their children looking on hungrily. On the next page there is a man dancing with a jar on his head at a village feast. Another sketch shows two women sitting on a rug smoking a waterpipe. In another drawing, a man is drinking from a clay jug. The water in the jug travels in a perfect arc from the spout to his mouth. In the villages today, they still drink water in this way.

Here we have the main idea in one sentence—the first sentence. Having stated the main idea, the writer goes on to give example after example of the "marvelous record." These examples are *supporting details*.

Conclusion. As a reader moves through a passage, grasping the main idea and supporting details, it is natural for him or her to begin to guess an ending or conclusion. Some paragraphs contain conclusions, others don't. It all depends on the purpose of the paragraph. For example, some paragraphs simply describe a process—how something is done. There is not much sense trying to draw a conclusion from such a paragraph.

There are two varieties of paragraphs with conclusions. In one, the conclusion is stated by the author. In the other, the conclusion is merely implied by the author, and it is up to you to draw it out.

Look for the conclusion that is stated in the following paragraph.

> A desert is an unusual place. A thunderstorm roars up in the distance. To cool off your sun-baked car, you head toward the storm, hoping for a few cool moments. You see the huge black cloud, the flashes of lightning, the black sheets of rain falling. Finally you are under the cloudburst, but you aren't getting rained on. Not a drop reaches your car. You stop the car, get out and look up. There, right above you, is the storm. Rain is pouring down toward you, and every bit of it evaporates before it gets close enough to wet you.

The conclusion is that though it rains above the desert, the rain doesn't reach the ground because it is evaporated by the hot, dry air.

In the next excerpt, the author strongly implies a conclusion, but does not state it directly.

> In fact, what I've said adds up to this: if you wish to enjoy your holiday in the Middle East, I suggest that you simply make up your mind that although you can get your money's worth if you're careful, and can make excellent purchases if you take your time, there are few bargains to be had. This is true of carpets, anyway.

From the paragraph above, we can draw the conclusion that carpets cannot be bought cheaply in the Middle East.

Looking for a conclusion puts you in the shoes of a detective. While reading, you have to think, "Where is the writer leading me? What's the conclusion?" And, like a detective, you must try to guess the conclusion, changing the guess as you get more and more information.

Clarifying Devices. Clarifying devices are words, phrases and techniques that a writer uses to make main ideas, sub-ideas and supporting details clear and interesting. By knowing some of these clarifying and controlling devices, you will be better able to recognize them in the passages you read. By recognizing them, you will be able to read with greater comprehension and speed.

Similes and Metaphors. Two literary devices that make a writer's ideas both clear and interesting are similes (SIM-a-lees) and metaphors (MET-a-fors). Both are used to make comparisons that add color and power to ideas. An example of a simile is *"She has a mind like a computer."* In this simile, a person's mind is compared to a computer. A simile always uses the word *like, as* or *than* to make a comparison. The metaphor, on the other hand, makes a direct comparison: *"Her mind is a computer."* Because metaphors are shorter and more direct, they are more forceful than similes. Writers use them to capture your attention, touch your emotions, and spark your imagination.

Transitional or Signal Words. The largest single group of clarifying devices, and the most widely used, are transitional or signal words. For example, here are some signal words that you see all the time: *first, second, next, last, finally.* A writer uses such words to keep ideas, steps in a process, or lists in order. Other transitional words include *in brief, in conclusion, above all, therefore, since, because* and *consequently.*

Organizational Patterns. Organizational patterns are also clarifying devices. One such pattern is the *chronological pattern*, in which events unfold in the order of time: one thing happens first, then another, and another, and so on. A time pattern orders events. The event may take place in five minutes or over a period of hundreds of years.

Vocabulary in Context. How accurate are you in using words you think you already know? Do you know that the word *exotic* means "a thing or person from a foreign country?" So, exotic flowers and exotic dancers are flowers and dancers from a foreign country. *Exotic* has been used incorrectly so often and for so long that it has developed a second meaning. Most people use *exotic* to mean "strikingly unusual, as in color or design."

Many people think that the words *imply* and *infer* mean the same thing. They do not. An author may imply, or suggest, something. The reader then infers what the author implied. In other words, to imply is to suggest an idea. To infer is to take meaning out.

It is easy to see what would happen to a passage if a reader skipped a word or two that he or she did not know, and imposed fuzzy meanings on a few others. The result would inevitably be a gross misunderstanding of the author's message. You will become a better reader if you learn the exact meanings and different shades of meaning of the words that are already familiar to you.

Answering the Main Idea Question

The main idea questions in this book are not the usual multiple-choice variety from which you must select the one correct statement. Rather, you are given three statements and are asked to select the statement that expresses the *main idea* of the passage, the statement that is *too narrow*, and the statement that is *too broad*. You have to work hard and actively to identify all three statements correctly. This new type of question teaches you to discriminate among seemingly equal statements.

To help you handle these questions, let's go behind the scenes to see how the main idea questions in this book were constructed. The true main idea statement was always written first. It had to be neat, succinct and positive. The main idea tells *who* or *what* the subject of the passage is. It also answers the question *does what?* or *is what?* Next, keeping the main idea statement in mind, the other two statements were written. They are variations of the main idea statement. The *too narrow* statement had to be in line with the main idea, but express only part of it. Likewise, the *too broad* statement had to be in line with the main idea, but be too general in scope.

Read the sample passage that starts below. Then follow the instructions in the box, to learn how to answer the main idea questions. The answer to each part of the question has been filled in for you. The score for each answer has also been marked.

Sample Passage

Did you know you can predict weather by watching swallows? When swallows fly high, you can expect fine weather. But when they fly low or close to the ground, rain is on the way. Swallows follow flies and gnats, which delight in warm currents of air. Warm air is lighter than cold air, and when the warm air currents are high in the sky, then there is less chance of rain. When the warm air is near the ground, then it is certain there will be rain.

1

	Answer	Score
Mark the *main idea* ⟶	**M**	15
Mark the statement that is *too broad* ⟶	**B**	5
Mark the statement that is *too narrow* ⟶	**N**	5

a. By watching swallows, a person can predict rain or fair weather.
   [This statement gathers all the important points. It gives a correct picture of the main idea in a brief way: (1) watching swallows, (2) predicting rain, and (3) predicting fair weather.]

   Ⓜ   15

b. When swallows fly high, there is less chance of rain.
   [This statement is correct, but it is too narrow. Only *part* of the main idea is stated. The prediction for rain is left out.]

   Ⓝ   5

c. People can predict weather by watching birds in flight.
   [This statement is too broad. It is stretching the point by saying "by watching birds in flight." According to the passage, only one kind of bird, swallows, can let us know whether or not it will rain.]

   Ⓑ   5

Getting the Most Out of This Book

The following steps could be called "tricks of the trade." Your teachers might call them "rules for learning." It doesn't matter what they are called. What does matter is that they work.

Think About the Title. A famous language expert told me a "trick" to use when I read. "The first thing to do is to read the title. Then spend a few moments thinking about it."

Writers spend much time thinking up good titles. They try to pack a lot of meaning into them. It makes sense, then, for you to spend a few seconds trying to dig out some meaning. These few moments of thought will give you a head start on a passage.

Thinking about the title can help you in another way, too. It helps you concentrate on a passage before you begin reading. Why does this happen? Thinking about the title fills your head full of thoughts about the passage. There's no room for anything else to get in to break concentration.

The Dot System. Here is a method that will speed up your reading. It also builds comprehension at the same time.

Spend a few moments with the title. Then read *quickly* through the passage. Next, without looking back, answer the six questions by placing a dot in the box next to each answer of your choice. The dots will be your "unofficial" answers. For the main idea question (question one), place your dot in the box next to the statement that you think is the main idea.

The dot system helps by making you think hard on your first, *fast* reading. The practice you gain by trying to grasp and remember ideas makes you a stronger reader.

The Check-Mark System. First, answer the main idea question. Follow the steps that are given above each set of statements for this question. Use a capital letter to mark your final answer to each part of the main idea question.

You have answered the other five questions with a dot. Now read the passage once more *carefully*. This time, mark your final answer to each question by placing a check mark (✓) in the box next to the answer of your choice. The answers with the check marks are the ones that will count toward your score.

The Diagnostic Chart. Now move your final answers to the Diagnostic Chart that starts on page 230.

Use the row of boxes beside *Passage 1* for the answers to the first passage. Use the row of boxes beside *Passage 2* for the answers to the second passage, and so on.

Write the letter of your answer to the left of the dotted line in each block.

Correct your answers using the Answer Key on pages 225–229. When scoring your answers, do *not* use an *x* for *incorrect* or a *c* for *correct*. Instead, use this method. If your choice is correct, make no mark in the right side of the answer block. If your choice is *incorrect*, write the letter of the correct answer to the right of the dotted line in the block.

Thus, the row of answers for each passage will show your incorrect answers. And it will also show the correct answers.

Your Total Comprehension Score. Go back to the passage you have just read. If you answered a question incorrectly, draw a line under the correct choice on the question page. Then write your score for each question on the line provided. Add the scores to get your total comprehension score. Enter that number in the box marked Total Score.

Graphing Your Progress. After you have found your total comprehension score, turn to the Progress Graph that begins on page 235. Write your score in the box under the number for the passage. Then put an **x** along the line above the box to show your total comprehension score. Join the **x**'s as you go. This will plot a line showing your progress.

Taking Corrective Action. Your incorrect answers give you a way to teach yourself how to read better. Take the time to study your wrong answers.

Go back to the questions. For each question you got wrong, read the correct answer (the one you have underlined) several times. With the correct answer in mind, go back to the passage itself. Read to see why the approved answer is better. Try to see where you made your mistake. Try to figure out why you chose a wrong answer.

The Steps in a Nutshell

Here's a quick review of the steps to follow. Following these steps is the way to get the most out of this book. Be sure you have read and understood all of the "To the Student" section on pages 13 through 21 before you start.

1. **Think About the Title of the Passage.** Try to get all the meaning the writer put into it.

2. **Read the Passage Quickly.**

3. **Answer the Questions, Using the Dot System.** Use dots to mark your unofficial answers. Don't look back at the passage.

4. **Read the Passage Again—Carefully.**

5. **Mark Your Final Answers.** Put a check mark (✓) in the box to note your final answer. Use capital letters for each part of the main idea question.

6. **Mark Your Answers on the Diagnostic Chart.** Record your final answers in the Diagnostic Chart that begins on page 230. Write your answers to the left of the dotted line in the answer blocks for the passage.

7. **Correct Your Answers.** Use the Answer Key on pages 225–229. If an answer is not correct, write the correct answer in the right side of the block, beside your wrong answer. Then go back to the question page. Place a line under the correct answer.

8. **Find Your Total Comprehension Score.** Find this by adding up the points you earned for each question. Enter the total in the box marked Total Score.

9. **Graph Your Progress.** Enter and plot your score on the graph that begins on page 235.

10. **Take Corrective Action.** Read your wrong answers. Read the passage once more. Try to figure out why you were wrong.

Count Dracula: Fact or Fiction?

A legend begun in 1897 has haunted people ever since. It is the story of Count Dracula, the vampire who drank human blood. How much of this legend is based on fact?

The real Count Dracula was a fifteenth-century prince who lived in Transylvania, which is in modern-day Rumania. At first, he was called Vlad IV. His father's name was Vlad Dracul, which meant *Vlad the Evil.* His son acquired the name of Dracula, or *Devil's Son.*

There are other similarities between the real and the legendary characters. The real Count Dracula is said to have been a cruel man. He showed no mercy to his enemies. When he captured them, he drove stakes into their bodies. This practice carried over to the fictional Dracula. It was a common belief that the only way to kill a vampire or a devil was to drive a stake into its heart, and that is how the fictional Dracula was finally killed.

Associated with the Dracula tale are vampire bats. They are not as dangerous as people believe. Bats require only a teaspoon of blood a day to survive. They seldom attack humans; they <u>subsist</u> mainly on the blood of cows and domestic animals. They are more threatening to humans as transmitters of disease, such as rabies.

Most legends are based on real events. Stories are passed along from one generation to another until they reach us, in a much changed form. A real event is like an original sound; a legend is an echo.

Main Idea	1		Answer	Score
		Mark the *main idea*	M	15
		Mark the statement that is *too broad*	B	5
		Mark the statement that is *too narrow*	N	5
		a. The real and the fictional Draculas had some common traits.	m	
		b. The story of Dracula is based on fact.	B N	
		c. The real Dracula was a cruel prince.	N	

Score 15 points for each correct answer. Score

Subject Matter

2 This passage is about
- ☐ a. vampire bats.
- ☒ b. the Dracula legend.
- ☐ c. Count Dracula as a cruel man.
- ☐ d. transmitters of disease. _____

Supporting Details

3 A vampire bat
- ☐ a. is very evil.
- ☐ b. can get tangled in one's hair.
- ☒ c. needs only a teaspoon of blood a day.
- ☐ d. attacks humans. _____

Conclusion

4 What conclusion has the author drawn from the facts?
- ☐ a. Dracula was speared with a lance.
- ☐ b. Dracula means "Devil's Son."
- ☒ c. Most legends are based on real events.
- ☐ d. Stories are passed from one generation to another. _____

Clarifying Devices

5 To compare the real and fictional Count Draculas, the author uses
- ☐ a. emotional appeals.
- ☒ b. facts.
- ☐ c. documents.
- ☐ d. arguments. _____

Vocabulary in Context

6 The word <u>subsist</u> means
- ☒ a. to live on.
- ☐ b. to kill.
- ☐ c. to wonder at.
- ☐ d. to ignore. _____

Add your scores for questions 1-6. Enter the total here and on the graph on page 235.

Total Score ☐

The Black Snow

On December 25, 1969, a black snow covered the shores of Lake Vattern, in Sweden. It seemed as though a giant oil slick had crept onto the land.

This sad event disturbed the natural <u>habits</u> of the wildlife. The hoofs of deer were covered with grease. Birds, their wings dripping with slime, could not fly. Rabbits slipped and fell on the oozy surface.

What caused this unusual incident? A group of scientists from Stockholm's Ecological Center set off at once to solve the mystery. After careful observation, they found the snow to be a mixture of harmful industrial pollutants. One of these was DDT, an insect-killing poison which is harmful to people, too. These substances had combined with water droplets in the air, and condensed as frozen rain. The rain, like a black dye, poured over snow that had fallen the night before.

The black rain seeped into clothing too, and proved impossible to remove. The black substance was so grainy that powerful detergents could not dissolve it.

This strange snow had not been an accident of nature. It was the fault of human beings.

Main Idea   1

	Answer	Score
Mark the *main idea* ⟶	M	15
Mark the statement that is *too broad* ⟶	B	5
Mark the statement that is *too narrow* ⟶	N	5

a. A black snow of harmful pollutants fell on a town in Sweden.   M   ____

b. Pollutants are dangerous to people and animals.   B   ____

c. Animals were hurt by the black snow.   N   ____

Score 15 points for each correct answer.   **Score**

Subject Matter   **2**   What is the writer talking about in this passage?

- ☐ a. Volcanic ash
- ☒ b. An insect-killing poison
- ☒ c. A black snow caused by industrial wastes
- ☐ d. The natural cycles of wildlife   _____

Supporting Details   **3**   DDT is

- ☐ a. a type of oil slick.
- ☐ b. a powerful detergent.
- ☐ c. a scientific institute.
- ☒ d. an insect-killing poison.   _____

Conclusion   **4**   The writer implies that

- ☐ a. the black snow was a product of nature.
- ☒ b. people should take greater care of the environment.
- ☐ c. natural cycles of wildlife should not be disturbed.
- ☐ d. the rain looked like black dye.   _____

Clarifying Devices   **5**   The writer uses the simile "The rain, like a black dye," to

- ☒ a. help the reader imagine how the snow looked.
- ☐ b. show the way words can be used to explain.
- ☐ c. get his own opinion into the reader's mind.
- ☐ d. persuade the reader to become ecology-minded.   _____

Vocabulary in Context   **6**   In this passage, <u>habits</u> means

- ☐ a. costumes.
- ☐ b. manners.
- ☒ c. behavior.
- ☐ d. customs.   _____

Add your scores for questions 1-6. Enter the total here and on the graph on page 235.   **Total Score** ☐

27

Knee-Deep in Water or Dust

In 1961 a car could drive across Lake Manyara in East Africa. Although normally more than 150 square miles in area, the lake did not have a drop of water in it. Yet, the next year, the lake rose so high that it drowned trees along the shore. Lake Manyara is filled by rivers that cascade down a steep cliff formed millions of years ago, when the earth's crust split and the western land sank several hundred feet. Water collects in the long valley formed by the rift, but the lake that is created has no outlet. Thus, in years of heavy rains the lake grows, rather than pouring the excess water into an outlet river. The lake is normally bordered in many places by open grasslands, but when it has rained long and hard it laps at the edge of the woods that grow between the grasslands and the rift wall.

Such changes in the level of the lake can be a matter of life or death for local wildlife. In times of severe drought, all suffer from thirst. But too much water can also be dangerous. During the wet years following 1961, the large, horned antelope known as the wildebeest could be found standing knee-deep in the water at the edge of the lake. When the grasslands were <u>submerged</u>, they had no other refuge from the woods, where lions could easily ambush and kill them. Only when the lake sank again could they fairly match their wariness and speed against the cunning and strength of the lions.

Main Idea	1		Answer	Score
		Mark the *main idea* ⟶	M	15
		Mark the statement that is *too broad* ⟶	B	5
		Mark the statement that is *too narrow* ⟶	N	5

a. Lake Manyara goes through great changes in water level.   m   _____

b. The amount of water in a lake can vary greatly.   B   _____

c. In wet years, Lake Manyara grows larger.   N   _____

Score 15 points for each correct answer.   **Score**

Subject Matter

2 This passage is mostly about
☐ a. how earthquakes create large lakes.
☒ b. the water level of Lake Manyara.
☐ c. the wildlife found in East Africa.
☐ d. the amount of rainfall in Africa.   _____

Supporting Details

3 Lake Manyara was formed
☐ a. in the year 1962.
☐ b. after a dam was built.
☐ c. when the climate changed.
☒ d. millions of years ago.   _____

Conclusion

4 Wildebeests are safest from lions when living
☒ a. on open grasslands.
☐ b. in thick brush.
☐ c. in swamps and marshes.
☐ d. on steep hillsides.   _____

Clarifying Devices

5 The writer begins this passage by using
☐ a. exaggeration.
☐ b. a metaphor.
☒ c. contrast.
☐ d. a definition.   _____

Vocabulary in Context

6 Submerged means
☐ a. joined together.
☐ b. invaded by enemies.
☒ c. covered with water.
☐ d. split into small pieces.   _____

Add your scores for questions 1-6. Enter the total here and on the graph on page 235.

Total Score ☐

Crack Shot

Outside the castle, the grim ritual was enacted again. A solitary man strolled across the field, his ragged clothing indicating his peasant status. The king appeared in the window, raised his rifle to his shoulder, took careful aim, and, at the crack of gunfire, the solitary figure crumpled to the dirt of the courtyard. Soon, the body would be carried away. The king turned away from the window, strangely satisfied that he could rest in peace another day.

Otto of Bavaria had <u>succeeded</u> to the throne in 1886, but he never ruled. For most of his life, he was confined to his room. There, he held conversations with the ghosts that lived in his dresser drawer. His family kept him from the exercise of his kingly powers, but the voices he heard in his room urged him to an awful deed. Each day, one peasant must die at his hands, to insure his well-being and his peace of mind. So, every day, the gruesome scene was repeated outside his window.

Each day, the guards carefully loaded the king's gun with blanks. Each day, a soldier dressed in rags would walk outside the castle, and would fall when the king fired his gun. In this way, the king's family humored his illness; the mad king went to his grave convinced he'd killed hundreds of innocent people.

Main Idea	1		Answer	Score
		Mark the *main idea* ⟶	**M**	15
		Mark the statement that is *too broad* ⟶	**B**	5
		Mark the statement that is *too narrow* ⟶	**N**	5

a. Mad King Otto's family deluded him by making him think that he'd killed the peasants, to satisfy his obsession. M _____

b. Throughout history, royalty have been humored in their desires. B _____

c. A soldier dressed in rags pretended to fall when shot at. N _____

Score 15 points for each correct answer.   **Score**

Subject Matter   **2** This passage is mostly about
    ☐ a. the decline of European royalty.
    ☒ b. the care of invalids.
    ☒ c. King Otto's madness.
    ☐ d. military service.   _____

Supporting Details   **3** Otto was kept from exercising authority by
    ☐ a. parliament.
    ☐ b. the judges.
    ☐ c. leaders of the army.
    ☒ d. his family.   _____

Conclusion   **4** It is believable that Otto could get away with shooting peasants because kings once
    ☒ a. ruled large territories.
    ☒ b. had the power of life and death over their subjects.
    ☐ c. were the wealthiest in their kingdom.
    ☐ d. passed the throne to their eldest sons.   _____

Clarifying Devices   **5** The author of this passage develops suspense by
    ☒ a. not disclosing the deception until the end.
    ☐ b. emphasizing the family's role.
    ☐ c. generalizing about monarchies.
    ☐ d. listing the king's unsavory characteristics.   _____

Vocabulary in Context   **6** The word <u>succeeded</u>, as used in this passage, means
    ☐ a. declined.
    ☒ b. inherited.
    ☐ c. financed.
    ☒ d. won.   _____

Add your scores for questions 1–6. Enter the total here and on the graph on page 235.

Total Score ☐

Neat and Clean

Birds spend so much time smoothing, cleaning and arranging their feathers that it's not surprising this behavior, called preening, is associated with pride and vanity. But stop a minute and think about what feathers do for a bird. Besides allowing it to fly, feathers keep the bird warm in the winter and cool in the summer, they shed water in the rain, and they are used to communicate with other birds of the same species. A bird with dirty or ruffled feathers will not live long.

Birds use their beaks to clean and straighten their feathers and to spread oil over them. They get the oil from special glands in their skin. The oil helps keep the feathers waterproof and flexible.

Birds also like to take baths to keep clean, and they don't always take them in water. Chickens, for instance, like nothing better than to scratch up some dust with their feet and then lie down and flap the dust all over their bodies. This probably helps get rid of <u>parasites</u> on their skin. A quick shake then sends the dust flying from their feathers, leaving them clean and comfortable.

Main Idea	1		Answer	Score
	Mark the *main idea* ——————→	M		15
	Mark the statement that is *too broad* ——→	B		5
	Mark the statement that is *too narrow* ——→	N		5
	a. Preening is very important to birds.	M		____
	b. Birds use their beaks to clean their feathers.	N		____
	c. The habits of birds are interesting.	B		____

Score 15 points for each correct answer.   **Score**

Subject Matter

2 This selection is about
- [ ] a. the vanity of birds.
- [ ] b. the pride of birds.
- [x] c. preening.
- [ ] d. methods of survival.   _____

Supporting Details

3 Which of the following is a supporting detail from the passage?
- [ ] a. Preening sharpens a bird's beak.
- [x] b. Only neat, well-oiled feathers will keep a bird dry in the rain.
- [ ] c. Dust baths help remove parasites from the bodies of all birds.
- [ ] d. Only a bird with well-cared-for feathers can escape predators.   _____

Conclusion

4 We can conclude that birds
- [ ] a. clean themselves because it's fun.
- [ ] b. only keep clean if they're forced to.
- [x] c. have an instinct for cleanliness.
- [ ] d. clean themselves because they're proud of their pretty feathers.   _____

Clarifying Devices

5 The writer used the word *probably* in the last paragraph to imply that
- [ ] a. the writer is certain of that much.
- [x] b. the exact reason is not yet known.
- [ ] c. parasites cause chickens to roll in the dust.
- [ ] d. chickens are not as clean as other birds.   _____

Vocabulary in Context

6 The word <u>parasites</u> means
- [ ] a. burrs that have stuck to the feathers of the chickens.
- [x] b. bugs living on and obtaining food from the chickens.
- [ ] c. scabs and sores that have developed on the bodies of the chickens.
- [ ] d. identification bands put on chickens by their owner.   _____

Add your scores for questions 1–6. Enter the total here and on the graph on page 235.   **Total Score** [ ]

33

6

The Barrymore Family

The Barrymores were a famous family of actors. There were two brothers and a sister. John, the youngest of the three, died first, in 1942, at the age of 60. He had been helping out at a rehearsal for a radio program, when he suddenly collapsed. He died at a hospital in Hollywood on May 29. His death was caused by a combination of respiratory and kidney ailments.

Lionel Barrymore, the oldest of the famous siblings, died of a heart attack in 1954, at the age of 77. He was at the home of a friend, near Los Angeles, reading *MacBeth* aloud, when the fatal attack struck. Lionel was overweight, and had suffered from heart problems in the past. He had broken his hip when he was 58, which confined him to a wheelchair. He was famous for, among many other things, his portrayal of Dr. Gillespie in the well-known series of Dr. Kildare films in the 1940s.

Ethel Barrymore was a year younger than Lionel, and died on June 18, 1959, at the age of 80. She had been an invalid for over a year when she died of heart disease. She also suffered from severe arthritis. Before she died, she was often visited by her good friend Katharine Hepburn, who described her as remaining beautiful and well groomed to the last. Her last words before she died were, "Is everybody happy? I want everybody to be happy. I know I'm happy!"

The Barrymores are buried together in Calvary Cemetery, Los Angeles.

Main Idea	1		Answer	Score
	Mark the *main idea* ⟶	M		15
	Mark the statement that is *too broad* ⟶	B		5
	Mark the statement that is *too narrow* ⟶	N		5
	a. The youngest Barrymore died first.	N		_____
	b. The Barrymores were a family of actors.	B		_____
	c. The three famous Barrymores died between 1942 and 1959.	M		_____

Score 15 points for each correct answer.   **Score**

Subject Matter

2 This passage deals mainly with
- [ ] a. the careers of three great actors.
- [ ] b. the story of a family of actors.
- [x] c. the deaths of the three Barrymores.
- [ ] d. Lionel Barrymore's death.   _____

Supporting Details

3 Lionel Barrymore died
- [ ] a. quickly and without pain.
- [ ] b. of kidney disease.
- [x] c. while reading *MacBeth*.
- [ ] d. in the arms of his wife.   _____

Conclusion

4 From reading this passage you can guess that
- [ ] a. Ethel Barrymore was helped greatly by the visits from Katherine Hepburn.
- [ ] b. Lionel Barrymore lived until 77 because of his experience as a doctor.
- [ ] c. John Barrymore collapsed due to stress caused by his work on the radio program.
- [x] d. Lionel Barrymore enjoyed reading plays aloud.   _____

Clarifying Devices

5 The writer used the quotation of Ethel Barrymore's last words in order to
- [ ] a. show us that she was a vibrant, positive person.
- [x] b. show us that she was not in touch with reality when she died.
- [ ] c. make us feel sad.
- [ ] d. make us think about our own happiness.   _____

Vocabulary in Context

6 Siblings means
- [ ] a. performers.
- [ ] b. brothers and sisters.
- [x] c. British citizens.
- [ ] d. team members.   _____

Add your scores for questions 1-6. Enter the total here and on the graph on page 235.   **Total Score** [ ]

7

Acrobatic Worms

When a moth or butterfly first hatches from the egg, it is in the worm-like larva stage. After a period of development, the larva spins a cocoon, and eventually a full-grown moth or butterfly emerges. But, who has ever heard of a moth emerging from a vegetable seed?

Well, there is a kind of moth that emerges from the Mexican jumping bean. The bean is actually a seed. It grows on a shrub that resembles the rubber tree. The flowers of this tree are put to a very unusual use. Huge swarms of moths, thick as clouds, hover over the blossoms and deposit their eggs among the petals. After a while, the eggs hatch into tiny caterpillars. The caterpillars bore into the hollow seeds of the plant. Once inside, the larvae survive by slowly eating the walls of their new homes—the inner tissue of the seeds!

When the worms chew the walls or wriggle inside the beans, the Mexican jumping beans begin to roll and hop. The larvae must stay away from direct sunlight, or the beans' centers become dangerously hot. So, when sun shines on a bean, the larva begins jumping inside until the bean rolls to a shady spot. The warmer it gets, the faster the bean rolls and hops.

The exact distance that a bean can jump has not been measured, but people who have watched these beans jump say it is quite impressive. Considering its size, the tiny larva is a powerful athlete.

Main Idea	1		Answer	Score
		Mark the *main idea* ⟶	M	15
		Mark the statement that is *too broad* ⟶	B	5
		Mark the statement that is *too narrow* ⟶	N	5
		a. Mexican jumping beans jump because tiny caterpillars inside them jump around.	M	_____
		b. Tiny moth caterpillars live inside the Mexican jumping beans.	N	_____
		c. The Mexican jumping bean is an intriguing seed.	B	_____

**Subject
Matter**

2 Another good title for this story might be

☒ a. The Mexican Jumping Bean.

☐ b. The Mystery of Hollow Seeds.

☐ c. A Cozy Home.

☐ d. Too Hot to Handle.   _____

**Supporting
Details**

3 The jumping bean hops faster when

☐ a. people watch.

☐ b. the larva is hungry.

☒ c. the sun shines on it.

☐ d. it's raining.   _____

Conclusion

4 How far a bean can jump remains a mystery
because

☐ a. people think it's magic.

☐ b. people don't understand the bean.

☐ c. the bean doesn't hop, it merely rolls.

☒ d. no one has measured the distance.   _____

**Clarifying
Devices**

5 In the third sentence, the author creates
interest by

☐ a. stating a scientific fact.

☒ b. asking a surprising question.

☐ c. warning the reader.

☐ d. appealing to the reader's sense of humor.   _____

**Vocabulary
in Context**

6 The word <u>considering</u> is closest in meaning to

☐ a. with the help of.

☐ b. knowing.

☒ c. taking into account.

☒ d. watching.   _____

**Add your scores for questions 1-6. Enter the
total here and on the graph on page 235.**   **Total
Score** ⬜

8

The Forgotten Mile

Can you imagine a painting that is a mile long? That is about the length of 500 cars put end to end. John Banvard, an American artist who lived between 1815 and 1891, devoted six years of his life to creating a gigantic mural.

In his painting, Banvard aimed to represent 1,200 miles of landscape along the Mississippi River. The first stage of his task involved detailed observation. He camped along the Mississippi banks for a year and produced countless sketches. To support himself during that time, the artist trapped animals.

When he returned to his home in Kentucky, Banvard faced a technical problem. How would he fit a mile of canvas into his studio? He found a way. He rolled the canvas onto a drum, and pulled out just as much as he needed at a time. He wound the completed portions onto another drum. He could never see all parts of the painting at the same time. Imagine writing a letter without being able to look back to the first lines!

The creation of the painting drew many spectators. Most people agreed that the work was very <u>meticulous</u>. The artist had crafted a detailed picture of the river banks.

The painting's fame spread across the United States and England. After the artist died, however, the painting could not be found. To this day, its whereabouts are unknown.

Main Idea	1		Answer	Score
		Mark the *main idea* ⟶	M	15
		Mark the statement that is *too broad* ⟶	B	5
		Mark the statement that is *too narrow* ⟶	N	5
		a. John Banvard created an unusual work of art.	B	____
		b. An American artist created a mile-long painting which has disappeared.	M	____
		c. John Banvard did a painting that depicted a long stretch of countryside along the Mississippi.	N	____

Score 15 points for each correct answer. **Score**

Subject Matter

2 This passage is about

- ☒ a. a very long painting.
- ☐ b. life on the Mississippi River.
- ☐ c. detailed observations.
- ☐ d. the hardships of an artist's life. _____

Supporting Details

3 Which of the following details adds interest to the topic?

- ☐ a. Banvard made countless sketches.
- ☒ b. The painting represents 1,200 miles of landscape.
- ☐ c. Banvard liked camping.
- ☐ d. The painting was detailed. _____

Conclusion

4 This passage suggests that

- ☐ a. the Mississippi River is beautiful.
- ☐ b. great paintings disappear.
- ☒ c. creating a giant mural is a tremendous undertaking.
- ☐ d. many artists are hunters. _____

Clarifying Devices

5 What technique does the writer use to help you imagine the feeling of not being able to see the whole painting at once?

- ☐ a. Dates
- ☐ b. Historical facts
- ☐ c. Humor
- ☒ d. A comparison _____

Vocabulary in Context

6 The word <u>meticulous</u> means

- ☐ a. long.
- ☒ b. detailed.
- ☐ c. huge.
- ☐ d. wide. _____

Add your scores for questions 1–6. Enter the total here and on the graph on page 235.

Total Score ☐

9

But It Tastes Good

East coast, west coast, and inland, one of the most popular, and often most costly, items in America's restaurants is the *homarus americanus*. What is this dish that is served so often, steamed or stuffed, in spite of its rather odd appearance? It is the ever popular lobster.

The lobster looks so strange and <u>hostile</u> that it's surprising anyone first had the nerve to try to eat it. Looking like a large insect, the lobster is actually a cousin of the spider. It has eight spindly legs covered with tiny hairs that detect sounds and smells. When sensing danger, the lobster runs backwards.

The lobster also detects food or approaching danger with its two pairs of antennae. When it can't avoid the danger, the lobster wields its two large claws in self-defense. As many lobster handlers have painfully discovered, it can be quite effective in snapping these pinchers.

The lobster's shell is usually a blotchy greenish-black. When it is cooked, it turns bright red. This hard shell, which serves as a barrier to the lobster's enemies, is also a barrier to the lobster-eater's delicious meal. The shell takes time and effort to crack, but the tender lobster meat is worth the work.

In spite of its lack of outward appeal and the difficulty of catching and eating it, the lobster was once almost too popular. For a time, the species was in danger of becoming extinct. But strict laws now require fishermen to release small lobsters and egg-bearing females. So, this strange-looking meal won't soon be disappearing from our tables.

Main Idea 1

	Answer	Score
Mark the *main idea* ⟶	**M**	15
Mark the statement that is *too broad* ⟶	**B**	5
Mark the statement that is *too narrow* ⟶	**N**	5

a. Popular foods sometimes have visually unappealing characteristics. [B] _____

b. The lobster is a popular food despite obstacles to its enjoyment. [M] _____

c. The lobster can be difficult to catch and eat. [N] _____

Score 15 points for each correct answer. **Score**

Subject Matter

2 The passage is mainly about
- ☐ a. eating in restaurants.
- ☐ b. cooking and eating lobsters.
- ☒ c. the lobster's characteristics and popularity.
- ☐ d. how the lobster almost became extinct.

_____

Supporting Details

3 According to the passage, the lobster changes color when it is
- ☐ a. shedding.
- ☐ b. in danger.
- ☐ c. removed from water.
- ☒ d. cooked.

_____

Conclusion

4 The last paragraph suggests that the lobster was threatened with extinction because
- ☐ a. laws made to protect the lobster have not worked.
- ☒ b. more lobsters were being caught than were being reproduced.
- ☐ c. the lobster population was decreasing for unknown reasons.
- ☐ d. fishermen were taking only egg-bearing females.

_____

Clarifying Devices

5 The writer tells us that the lobster looks like an insect and is related to the spider in order to
- ☐ a. show why the lobster is popular.
- ☒ b. explain why the lobster behaves as it does.
- ☒ c. indicate why its popularity as a food may be surprising.
- ☐ d. explain why it has antennae.

_____

Vocabulary in Context

6 As used in the passage, hostile is closest in meaning to
- ☒ a. unfriendly.
- ☐ b. timid.
- ☐ c. cautious.
- ☐ d. ugly.

_____

Add your scores for questions 1–6. Enter the total here and on the graph on page 235.   **Total Score** ☐

10

Stronger Than an Elephant?

The jungles of southeast Asia are home to the largest snakes in the world, the regal, or reticulated, pythons. These snakes can grow to be more than thirty feet long, and are among the strongest animals in the world. They do not, however, actually crush their prey. The python catches its victims by waiting in <u>ambush</u>, its long spotted body looking like a vine or tree trunk. When a monkey or pig comes close, the python strikes by quickly wrapping several coils of its body around the animal. Then the snake slowly tightens the coils every time the animal breathes out, until it has suffocated its prey.

The most amazing part of the python's hunting method is the way in which it eats its prey, for it has no arms or legs, and its teeth, although sharp, are quite thin and delicate. The trick is that the snake can stretch its neck to many times its usual diameter, it can move the two halves of its lower jaw separately from each other, and its teeth curve backward. Starting at the prey's head, the python actually pulls itself over its victim by sliding one jaw forward and sinking in the teeth on that side, and using that as an anchor to pull the other jaw forward until the entire body has been swallowed.

		Answer	Score
Main Idea	**1**		
	Mark the *main idea* ⟶	M	15
	Mark the statement that is *too broad* ⟶	B	5
	Mark the statement that is *too narrow* ⟶	N	5

a. After pythons squeeze their victims to death, they devour them by dragging them into their mouths and swallowing them whole. [m] _____

b. Pythons squeeze their prey to death by coiling their bodies around them. [N] _____

c. Pythons have unusual and interesting living habits. [B] _____

Score 15 points for each correct answer.   **Score**

Subject
Matter

2 This passage focuses on the

☐ a. python's size.

☐ b. most poisonous snakes.

☒ c. python's hunting method.

☐ d. snake family.   _____

Supporting
Details

3 The snake kills its prey

☐ a. with poisonous venom.

☐ b. by biting it.

☒ c. by suffocating it.

☐ d. by swallowing it.   _____

Conclusion

4 This passage does <u>not</u> imply that pythons

☐ a. eat many different kinds of animals.

☐ b. are strong.

☐ c. have an unusual mouth structure.

☒ d. are poisonous snakes.   _____

Clarifying
Devices

5 The author gives the readers a good
understanding of pythons through the use of

☐ a. metaphors.

☒ b. description.

☐ c. comparison.

☐ d. examples.   _____

Vocabulary
in Context

6 An <u>ambush</u> is a

☐ a. branch.

☐ b. hidden bush.

☒ c. surprise attack.

☐ d. disguise.   _____

**Add your scores for questions 1–6. Enter the
total here and on the graph on page 235.**

Total
Score ☐

11

Keeping a Promise

The movie *Butch Cassidy and the Sundance Kid* portrayed Butch Cassidy as a charming and <u>sympathetic</u> fellow. Apparently, the movie's portrayal of Cassidy was true to life. The robberies that Cassidy's gang, the Wild Bunch, committed often had a Robin Hood quality; that is, they did not rob the poor, but only the rich.

Butch himself never killed anyone. His only known gunfight took place in Bolivia. He was killed in it. He preferred to surprise and over-awe, rather than to kill or hurt. Nevertheless, he was, in fact, fast and accurate with a gun. He could fast-draw and hit a playing card nailed to a distant tree, or shatter a bottle tossed into the air.

Stories about Butch reveal his unusual charm and personal honesty, which remained intact even as he went about committing robberies. For instance, the only time Butch was ever captured and convicted, he talked his jailers into allowing him to go out on the town before being locked up. He came back the next day as promised.

After a year in jail, Cassidy's charm once again helped him. He was set free by the governor of Wyoming after promising to leave Wyoming's cattle and banks alone. Butch again kept his promise. It is true that he never held up any banks or ran off with any cattle in Wyoming, but he started holding up and robbing the railroads in Wyoming, for railroads weren't mentioned in the agreement with the governor.

Main Idea	1		Answer	Score
	Mark the *main idea* →		M	15
	Mark the statement that is *too broad* →		B	5
	Mark the statement that is *too narrow* →		N	5
	a. The Wild Bunch was like Robin Hood's gang.		N	___
	b. Butch Cassidy was a charming outlaw who always kept his word.		M	___
	c. Many crimes were committed in the Old West.		B	___

Subject Matter

2 This passage is mostly about

- ☐ a. the governor of Wyoming.
- ☐ b. the movie *Butch Cassidy and the Sundance Kid.*
- ☒ c. Butch Cassidy.
- ☐ d. jailers of the Old West. _____

Supporting Details

3 Why did the jailers let Butch out?

- ☐ a. They were not well trained.
- ☐ b. They were old friends of Butch.
- ☒ c. Butch talked them into it.
- ☐ d. They knew Butch was not guilty. _____

Conclusion

4 Cassidy's shooting skill can be described as

- ☐ a. below average.
- ☐ b. inconvenient.
- ☒ c. accurate.
- ☐ d. deadly. _____

Clarifying Devices

5 The author develops the main idea by

- ☐ a. comparing the movie with Butch's real life.
- ☒ b. telling stories about Butch.
- ☒ c. recalling people's descriptions of Butch.
- ☐ d. setting forth damaging evidence. _____

Vocabulary in Context

6 Sympathetic is used to mean

- ☐ a. sorrowful.
- ☐ b. talkative.
- ☒ c. likable.
- ☐ d. two-faced. _____

Add your scores for questions 1-6. Enter the total here and on the graph on page 235.

Total Score ☐

12

The Fastest Land Animal

The cheetah is a very unusual kind of cat. This long-legged animal lives on the short-grass plains of Africa, in the same areas as the lordly lion and the smaller, but very powerful, leopard. In contrast to these and most other cats, which hunt by leaping from ambush, the cheetah runs down its prey. In fact, the cheetah is the fastest of all land mammals; it can sprint at up to sixty miles per hour. Its claws are used more for running than for clinging to prey, and unlike other cats, the cheetah cannot <u>retract</u> its claws.

Although it is an incredibly fast predator, the cheetah is no threat to humans. Oddly enough, it will not attack people even in self-defense. This is yet another way in which the cheetah differs from its relatives, the lion and the leopard. Both these cats are very dangerous when cornered, and have even been known to kill people for food. The cheetah's speed and unaggressive nature, however, have not saved it from the guns of human hunters. Its black-spotted coat is in great demand for fur coats, and only where it is protected in parks can people hope to see this beautiful cat running free.

Main Idea   **1**

	Answer	Score
Mark the *main idea* →	M	15
Mark the statement that is *too broad* →	B	5
Mark the statement that is *too narrow* →	N	5

a. Unlike most other cats, cheetahs run down their prey.   [N] _____

b. The cat family includes many different species.   [B] _____

c. Cheetahs are beautiful and unusual African cats.   [M] _____

Score 15 points for each correct answer.   **Score**

Subject Matter

2 This passage is mostly concerned with
- ☐ a. why fur coats are popular.
- ☐ b. the hunting behavior of African cats.
- ☒ c. unusual facts about the cheetah.
- ☐ d. why cheetahs are such dangerous predators.   _____

Supporting Details

3 According to this passage, the cheetah's fur
- ☐ a. is long and thick.
- ☒ b. has black spots.
- ☐ c. has a golden color.
- ☐ d. is not very valuable.   _____

Conclusion

4 Lions and leopards probably hunt from ambush because
- ☐ a. they hunt very small animals.
- ☐ b. they live in thick forests.
- ☒ c. they cannot outrun their prey.
- ☐ d. they are very lazy animals.   _____

Clarifying Devices

5 The writer's use of the phrase "oddly enough" suggests that the cheetah's reluctance to attack people is
- ☐ a. noble.
- ☒ b. surprising.
- ☐ c. intelligent.
- ☐ d. stupid.   _____

Vocabulary in Context

6 When a cat <u>retracts</u> its claws it
- ☒ a. pulls them in.
- ☐ b. sharpens them.
- ☐ c. straightens them.
- ☐ d. chews on them.   _____

Add your scores for questions 1-6. Enter the total here and on the graph on page 235.   **Total Score** ☐

13

Medicine for the American Indian

The Indian medicine man might have been more appropriately called a plant doctor. To the Indian, medicine was not so much a science as it was an art. Indian herb doctors would sometimes go to their graves without revealing their secrets of the healing powers of plants.

Medicine men often journeyed several days from their camps to search for soothing herbs and roots such as prickly ash, ginseng, pine gum and wintergreen. Care was always taken to make the proper sacrifices to the plant <u>spirits</u>.

Plants were never gathered carelessly or with haste. Ceremony preceded each harvest. Fires were built and tobacco was burned as sacrificial incense. A song was sung as each plant was gently pulled from the ground.

The herbs were prepared and stored with as much care as was taken when they were harvested. They were dried, cut and placed in special leather bags. Only certain Indians were allowed to handle the sacred medicines.

Unfortunately, some of the herbs had more magic in them than medicine. But many plants were effective in curing all kinds of ills. For example, boneset tea and prickly ash bark were prescribed for colds and fevers. Stomach troubles were often treated with wintergreen and slippery elm. Sassafras roots soothed the discomfort of mosquito bites. Fortunately for the early Indians, contagious diseases were almost nonexistent until the Europeans came to North America.

Main Idea 1

	Answer	Score
Mark the *main idea* ⟶	**M**	15
Mark the statement that is *too broad* ⟶	**B**	5
Mark the statement that is *too narrow* ⟶	**N**	5

a. Indian medicine men gathered plants to treat sickness.   m [M] _____

b. Indians knew a great deal about people.   B [B] _____

c. Indians gathered herbs with great ceremony.   N [N] _____

Score 15 points for each correct answer. **Score**

Subject Matter

2 Another good title for this passage would be
- ☐ a. Indian Superstitions.
- ☒ b. The Indian Art of Medicine.
- ☒ c. Plants and Their Uses.
- ☐ d. An Apple a Day Keeps the Plant Doctor Away.

_____

Supporting Details

3 Plants were picked only after a brief
- ☐ a. rest.
- ☒ b. meal.
- ☐ c. journey.
- ☒ d. ceremony.

_____

Conclusion

4 This passage suggests that Indians believed in
- ☒ a. the magical powers of plants.
- ☐ b. taking care of old folks.
- ☒ c. powerful tree gods.
- ☐ d. the laws of medicine.

_____

Clarifying Devices

5 The author discusses the positive effects of Indian herbal medicines by
- ☐ a. telling a story.
- ☒ b. offering sound arguments.
- ☒ c. giving examples.
- ☐ d. narration.

_____

Vocabulary in Context

6 Another word for <u>spirit</u> might be
- ☒ a. alcohol.
- ☐ b. enthusiasm.
- ☒ c. god.
- ☐ d. ghost.

_____

Add your scores for questions 1-6. Enter the total here and on the graph on page 235.

Total Score ☐

49

14

Strength in Numbers

The lion may be the most famous of all the predators of Africa, but one of the most fascinating is the wild dog. Wild dogs are fairly small, averaging seventy pounds, with round, fanlike ears that look too big for their heads. They have shaggy brown coats with scattered patches of white. One of these animals by itself looks harmless or even comical. But when they band together, in packs of up to forty, the wild dogs become dangerous predators that tirelessly run down and kill animals that are many times their own size.

Wild dogs have to be good hunters in order to feed their large families: a single female can have as many as sixteen pups at a time. But usually only one female in a pack breeds at a time, and all the pack members help to care for the young. At first, the pups feed on their mother's milk. Then the other dogs begin to bring back meat from the kill, carrying it in their stomachs and throwing it up when the pups come running to them to beg for food. Finally, the young dogs begin to go along on hunts. At this time one of the most striking differences between wild dogs and lions can be seen. When a pride of lions makes a kill, the adult males always eat their fill first. But the wild dogs let the pups feed first, even when they are still too young to really help in making the kill.

Main Idea	1		Answer	Score
		Mark the *main idea* ⟶	M	15
		Mark the statement that is *too broad* ⟶	B	5
		Mark the statement that is *too narrow* ⟶	N	5

a. The wild dogs of Africa can kill even large animals. **N** _____

b. There are many interesting predators in Africa. **B** _____

c. African wild dogs are fascinating predators. **M** _____

Score 15 points for each correct answer.   **Score**

Subject Matter

2 Another good title for this passage would be

☒ a. Africa's Wild Dogs.

☐ b. Killers of the Plains.

☐ c. Predators of Africa.

☐ d. The Greedy Lion. _____

Supporting Details

3 Wild dogs are dangerous predators because they

☐ a. are very fierce.

☒ b. hunt in large packs.

☐ c. are very intelligent.

☐ d. have unusually large litters. _____

Conclusion

4 You can assume that if all the females in a large pack had pups,

☐ a. only the father would help feed them.

☐ b. lions would find and kill them.

☐ c. the mothers would fight each other.

☒ d. most of the pups would starve. _____

Clarifying Devices

5 Lions are mentioned in this passage for

☒ a. comparison.

☐ b. excitement.

☐ c. comic relief.

☐ d. accuracy. _____

Vocabulary in Context

6 <u>Striking</u> is used to mean

☒ a. remarkable.

☐ b. terrifying.

☐ c. important.

☐ d. trivial. _____

Add your scores for questions 1-6. Enter the total here and on the graph on page 235.

Total Score ☐

51

15

A Year to Remember

At the Battle of Hastings, on October 14, 1066, the English confronted the Norman invaders. On one side waved the flag of Harold II, King of England, on which was stitched, in gold thread and gems, the figure of a knight in arms. Harold's knights stood around him, shields and war axes in hand, their backs to the great Wald Forest. Before them was a low valley, and at the <u>summit</u> of the next hill stood the knights and archers of the Norman duke, William.

Suddenly the Normans shouted their war cry, "God help us!" and the English responded with their own, "God's Rod (Cross)." The Normans sent a slew of arrows toward the English stronghold, as their horsemen charged up the hill. But the English locked their shields together to form a wall, and, thus protected from arrows, caused great destruction with their axes among the Norman cavalry. But then Duke William made a feint as if he would retreat. Hot for victory, some of the Englishmen left their safe hilltop and gave chase, only to be ridden down and slain in the valley. From noon to dusk the Normans sent their hail of arrows, and slowly they cut away the English ranks. At last King Harold fell with a fatal wound, and the Norman conquest of England had begun. Thus started the reign of William the Conqueror.

Main Idea   **1**

	Answer	Score
Mark the *main idea* ⟶	M	15
Mark the statement that is *too broad* ⟶	B	5
Mark the statement that is *too narrow* ⟶	N	5

a. The English fought the Normans in the Battle of Hastings. N _____

b. The Battle of Hastings was a turning point in England's history. M B _____

c. Duke William of the Normans killed King Harold and conquered England in the Battle of Hastings. B M _____

Subject Matter

2 This passage is mainly about
- ☐ a. strategic fighting between neighboring countries.
- ☐ b. conquerors who wanted more land and power.
- ☒ c. the battle between King Harold and Duke William.
- ☐ d. a civil war between the peasants and the landowners.   _____

Supporting Details

3 According to the passage, the battle lasted
- ☐ a. all day, from morning to night.
- ☐ b. from morning to noon.
- ☐ c. until all the English were killed.
- ☒ d. all afternoon.   _____

Conclusion

4 We can infer from the passage that
- ☒ a. Duke William was a smart fighter.
- ☐ b. England is a small country.
- ☐ c. the Englishmen were not brave.
- ☐ d. the Norman invaders were barbarians.   _____

Clarifying Devices

5 The writer tells the story by
- ☐ a. using a dry, objective narrative style.
- ☒ b. describing the causes and consequences of the battle.
- ☐ c. encouraging us to sympathize with the English.
- ☒ d. first setting the scene, then describing the action.   _____

Vocabulary in Context

6 Summit most closely means
- ☐ a. valley.
- ☐ b. foot.
- ☐ c. bottom.
- ☒ d. top.   _____

Add your scores for questions 1-6. Enter the total here and on the graph on page 235.   **Total Score** ☐

16

Rats

Rats! Through all of human history, they have been a curse and a plague to people. They eat or spoil crops of grain and rice before they can be harvested, or while they are in storage. In India, where millions of people go hungry, there are ten times as many rats as people. Rats devour half of the available food. Rats will also attack birds and animals, from frogs and chicks to geese and young calves. They have even destroyed dams and buildings by burrowing through or under them, and have started fires by chewing on electrical wiring.

The most terrible destruction caused by rats, however, has come from the diseases they carry. In the fourteenth century, rats caused the death of one-third of the world's human population by transmitting the dreadful Black Plague that ravaged Europe.

Ironically, it is in fighting diseases that rats have been most useful to humanity. Thousands of specially bred rats are used in research laboratories every year to test medicines which can possibly be used to prolong and improve human life. Some laboratory rats are even used to test new methods of <u>eliminating</u> their cousins, the wild rats.

Main Idea	1		Answer	Score
	Mark the *main idea* ⟶	M		15
	Mark the statement that is *too broad* ⟶	B		5
	Mark the statement that is *too narrow* ⟶	N		5

a. Diseases carried by rats have killed many people.   N ____

b. Wild rats cause many problems for mankind.   M B ____

c. Animal pests destroy human lives and property.   B M ____

Score 15 points for each correct answer.   **Score**

Subject Matter

2 Another good title for this passage would be
- [ ] a. The Black Plague.
- [x] b. Enemy of Humanity.
- [ ] c. Common Animal Pests.
- [ ] d. Causes of World Hunger.   _____

Supporting Details

3 The worst disaster caused by rats was the
- [ ] a. starving of millions in India.
- [ ] b. flooding of Holland by the sea.
- [x] c. spreading of the Plague in Europe.
- [ ] d. losing of thousands of homes by fire.   _____

Conclusion

4 Which of the following is implied but not stated in this passage?
- [x] a. Rats eat their prey alive.
- [ ] b. Rats carry the Black Plague.
- [ ] c. Rats are completely worthless.
- [x] d. Rats have caused floods.   _____

Clarifying Devices

5 The writer mentions the Black Plague as
- [x] a. an example.
- [ ] b. a symbol.
- [ ] c. a warning.
- [ ] d. a myth.   _____

Vocabulary in Context

6 When something is <u>eliminated</u> it is
- [ ] a. identified.
- [x] b. removed.
- [ ] c. discovered.
- [ ] d. trained.   _____

Add your scores for questions 1-6. Enter the total here and on the graph on page 235.

Total Score [   ]

17

First National Monument

Devils Tower, the first national monument in America, could almost be mistaken for the stump of an enormous tree. Its sheer rock sides sweep up from a broad base until they cut off abruptly at the flat summit. Rising more than 1,000 feet above the gently rolling plains of Wyoming, this massive column of rock looks as though it was carried there from a different time and place.

In a sense it was. It is a <u>relic</u> of the past, when the molten rock of the earth's core forced its way to the surface to form the throat of a volcano. As the centuries passed the rock cooled and hardened, shrinking and cracking into long columns. Born in fire and fury, Devils Tower was then shaped by the slow, gentle work of wind and water. The outer layers of the volcano were worn away, until the hard core stood completely exposed.

Small wonder that an Indian legend described Devils Tower as being formed by supernatural powers. The legend says that when seven girls were attacked by bears, they took refuge on top of a small rock and appealed to the Rock God for help. The god caused the rock to grow and to lift the girls far above the ground, while its sides were scored by the claws of the angry bears. Even today, says the legend, the girls can be seen above the towering rock, as seven shining stars in the night sky.

Main Idea   1

	Answer	Score
Mark the *main idea* ⟶	M	15
Mark the statement that is *too broad* ⟶	B	5
Mark the statement that is *too narrow* ⟶	N	5

a. Devils Tower, which is the exposed core of an ancient volcano, was the first national monument in America. *M* [N] ____

b. Devils Tower was first formed many centuries ago. *N* [B] ____

c. One example of a natural rock formation is Devils Tower. *B* [M] ____

Score 15 points for each correct answer.   Score

Subject Matter

2 This passage is mostly about
- ☐ a. Indian legends.
- ☐ b. petrified trees.
- ☒ c. Devils Tower.
- ☐ d. volcanos.

_____

Supporting Details

3 What caused the volcano's outer layer to disappear?
- ☐ a. Violent storms
- ☐ b. The cooling of the core
- ☐ c. An earthquake
- ☒ d. Wind and water

_____

Conclusion

4 Devils Tower looks out of place because it
- ☐ a. was built by the Indians as a religious monument.
- ☒ b. is surrounded by open plains, with no other rock formations nearby.
- ☐ c. is much older than other nearby mountains.
- ☐ d. was scored by the claws of angry bears.

_____

Clarifying Devices

5 The author describes Devils Tower as looking like the stump of an enormous tree in order to
- ☒ a. help the reader visualize its appearance.
- ☐ b. explain how an Indian legend was started.
- ☐ c. suggest that it was once a living object.
- ☐ d. emphasize how deceptive appearances can be.

_____

Vocabulary in Context

6 As used in this passage, <u>relic</u> refers to a
- ☐ a. holy place.
- ☒ b. leftover part.
- ☐ c. piece of old art.
- ☐ d. reminder.

_____

Add your scores for questions 1-6. Enter the total here and on the graph on page 235.

Total Score ☐

18

The Century Flower

Imagine a plant that blooms only once every hundred years! During the last hundred years, technology has produced the plane and the rocket. People have traveled through space, reached the moon, and measured the distance to a star. Television, telephone and radio have been invented. Through all this time, the ma-dake bamboo of Japan, a "century plant," has flowered but once.

The Japanese people greet the <u>phenomenon</u> of the plant's flowering with sadness. The economic life of the country people depends to a great extent upon the ma-bamboo. It is used in making paper, creating art, building houses and for a myriad of other purposes. Unfortunately, once the plant blooms, it dies. The Japanese people mourn the death of these plants, just as an American farmer would mourn the death of a wheatfield.

Miles of bamboo forests wither at the same time. This is because a forest consists of a single generation of plants. Plants in a generation go through the various stages of development together.

Most other plants and flowers produce seeds and fruit. The ma-bamboo doesn't. It is unique. It sends out roots to perpetuate itself. When the bamboo blossoms, even the roots die. Ten years must pass before new roots take hold.

The bamboo last flowered in 1960. In most parts of Japan, it will not blossom again until 2060. Like Halley's Comet, it is a rare, natural occurrence, to be seen only once in a lifetime, if one is born at the right time.

Main Idea 1

	Answer	Score
Mark the *main idea* ⟶	M	15
Mark the statement that is *too broad* ⟶	B	5
Mark the statement that is *too narrow* ⟶	N	5
a. The ma-bamboo blossoms but once in a hundred years.	M	___
b. Though the ma-bamboo's blossoms are pretty, they produce sadness.	N	___
c. The ma-bamboo is an unusual plant.	B	___

Score 15 points for each correct answer.   **Score**

Subject Matter

2 The subject of this passage is

☐ a. a sad event.

☒ b. the ma-bamboo.

☐ c. changes within a century.

☐ d. unique flowers.   _____

Supporting Details

3 Ten years must pass before

☐ a. the flower dies.

☐ b. the flower blooms.

☒ c. new roots take hold.

☐ d. Halley's Comet returns.   _____

Conclusion

4 The ma-bamboo is important to the Japanese because it is

☐ a. rare.

☐ b. beautiful.

☒ c. used for many purposes.

☐ d. self perpetuating.   _____

Clarifying Devices

5 In the first paragraph, the writer creates interest in the subject by using

☐ a. precise arguments.

☐ b. amusing narratives.

☐ c. a biased opinion.

☒ d. contrasts of time.   _____

Vocabulary in Context

6 The word <u>phenomenon</u> means

☐ a. surprise.

☒ b. special occurrence.

☐ c. horror.

☐ d. fearful sight.   _____

Add your scores for questions 1–6. Enter the total here and on the graph on page 235.   **Total Score** ☐

19

Ancient Doctoring

Until a century ago, bloodletting was used to treat many <u>ailments</u>. Dating back to before the time of Christ, the treatment involved letting a type of worm, called a leech, suck blood from the patient. People believed that there were liquids called humors in the body, and that these determined a person's personality and health. Bloodletting, they thought, restored a balance to these humors.

At this time, little was known of the workings of the human body. But people did know, at least, that the same liquid, blood, flowed throughout all of their bodies. They knew it was a vital substance, for loss of any great amount of it meant certain death. Thus, they concluded that all diseases were carried in the bloodstream, and that if the body was relieved of bad blood, health would return. Bloodletting, however, came to be used as a cure-all. Women were bled to keep them from blushing. Members of the clergy were bled to prevent them from thinking sinful and worldly thoughts.

From the eleventh to the eighteenth centuries, barbers were the people to go to if you needed to be bled, as well as for a shave. This duty explains the significance of the traditional red and white striped barber's pole. The white stripes stand for bandages, and the red stripes for blood.

Main Idea 1

	Answer	Score
Mark the *main idea* ⟶	M	15
Mark the statement that is *too broad* ⟶	B	5
Mark the statement that is *too narrow* ⟶	N	5

a. Bloodletting was once used as the traditional method of curing all illnesses. 　M ____

b. People thought blood contained liquids called humors. 　N ____

c. People a century ago didn't know much about medicine. 　B ____

Score 15 points for each correct answer.   **Score**

Subject Matter

2 This passage is concerned with
- ☐ a. healthy people and doctors.
- ☒ b. bleeding as a cure-all.
- ☐ c. barbers of long ago.
- ☐ d. leeches with special jobs to do.   _____

Supporting Details

3 The red and white stripes on barber poles symbolize
- ☒ a. sin and redemption.
- ☒ b. the bleeding ritual.
- ☐ c. women who are nurses.
- ☐ d. humors in the body.   _____

Conclusion

4 Why is bloodletting no longer considered a cure-all?
- ☒ a. Because more is known about the workings of the human body
- ☐ b. Because leeches were outlawed
- ☐ c. Because barbers were too busy cutting hair
- ☐ d. Because today we know that blood is necessary for health   _____

Clarifying Devices

5 In the second paragraph, the word *thus* could be replaced by the word
- ☐ a. when.
- ☒ b. however.
- ☐ c. if.
- ☒ d. so.   _____

Vocabulary in Context

6 Ailments means
- ☐ a. cures.
- ☐ b. women.
- ☒ c. diseases.
- ☐ d. medicines.   _____

Add your scores for questions 1-6. Enter the total here and on the graph on page 235.

Total Score [ ]

20

How to Attract a Female

Ladies seem to really go for big guys with deep voices—even when the lady is a toad and the guy is sitting in a pond croaking. A scientist studying Fowler's toads in a North Carolina pond found that the biggest males were the most successful in attracting females. Since toads <u>court</u> at night, and often in the rain, it seemed unlikely that females could judge the size of their swains by sight alone. But it is a well-known fact that the bigger a toad is, the deeper its voice is. Sure enough, when a group of females was given a choice between approaching a high-pitched call and a low-pitched call played on a tape recorder, they all headed for the lowest voice. They pick out the big guys by their voices.

There is one complication, however. A toad's body temperature stays at the same level as the air or water surrounding it—and the colder the toad, the deeper its voice. So when the water is colder than the air, a male in the pond can sound bigger than he really is, giving him a definite advantage over a similar toad on the shore. Unfortunately for the little guys, though, the big toads are also stronger and chase their smaller competitors out of the water, hogging the best spots for themselves.

Main Idea	1		Answer	Score
	Mark the *main idea* ⟶		M	15
	Mark the statement that is *too broad* ⟶		B	5
	Mark the statement that is *too narrow* ⟶		N	5

a. Female toads choose their mates in the dark. N M _____

b. A female toad uses sound to guide her to a large male. M N _____

c. Some scientists study how female animals choose males. B _____

Score 15 points for each correct answer.   **Score**

Subject Matter

2 This passage deals with

☐ a. the reason scientists study animal behavior.

☒ b. how female toads choose a mate.

☐ c. the best way to catch toads.

☐ d. why toads are cold-blooded animals.   _____

Supporting Details

3 Whether a toad's call is high-pitched or low-pitched depends on

☐ a. who it is calling to.

☐ b. how healthy it is.

☐ c. how old it is.

☒ d. its body temperature.   _____

Conclusion

4 According to this passage, a male toad should always prefer to call from a place that is

☐ a. high.

☐ b. wet.

☒ c. cold.

☐ d. warm.   _____

Clarifying Devices

5 The writer supports the main idea by using

☐ a. amusing anecdotes.

☐ b. well-known facts of human behavior.

☐ c. an appeal to common sense.

☒ d. the results of experiments.   _____

Vocabulary in Context

6 In this passage <u>court</u> means to

☒ a. mate.

☐ b. congregate.

☐ c. judge.

☐ d. travel.   _____

Add your scores for questions 1-6. Enter the total here and on the graph on page 235.

Total Score ☐

21

The Telltale Beam

If you saw the popular film *Raiders of the Lost Ark*, you will remember the small opening in the roof of a tomb, which allowed a beam of sunlight to strike a spot on the tomb's floor at a certain time each day. Well, there is a similar device in a real cathedral in Italy, although its purpose is not quite as exciting as the one in the film.

In 1420, seventy-two years before Columbus discovered America, a great Italian architect, Filippo Brunelleschi, built a cathedral in the city of Florence. He left a small opening in the dome, which allowed a slender beam of sunlight to shine through onto the church floor. Built into the floor was a small metal plate. Every year, on the twenty-first of June, the beam of sunlight was supposed to fall on this metal plate— and that it has done, every year for over five hundred and sixty years!

Why was the cathedral designed with this special <u>feature</u>? Well, the church was built in a place that was marshy, which means that the ground was very unstable, like mud. If it ever happened that the light beam did not strike the special metal plate on June 21, it would mean that the church had shifted, or moved out of place, on its base. People would know that they had to fix the cathedral so it wouldn't fall, or they would have time to make sure everyone nearby was safe in case it collapsed.

Main Idea	1		Answer	Score
	Mark the *main idea* →		**M**	15
	Mark the statement that is *too broad* →		**B**	5
	Mark the statement that is *too narrow* →		**N**	5

a. Brunelleschi built the cathedral on marshy ground. N [B] ____

b. One must be careful when building cathedrals. B [N] ____

c. The cathedral in Florence was designed with a special feature that warned if the building shifted. M [M] ____

Score 15 points for each correct answer.   **Score**

Subject Matter

2 This passage deals mostly with
- [ ] a. *Raiders of the Lost Ark.*
- [ ] b. a famous Italian architect.
- [x] c. a cathedral in Florence.
- [ ] d. metal floor plates.   _____

Supporting Details

3 The special device was added because
- [ ] a. the church might fall in an earthquake.
- [x] b. it could warn people if the cathedral had moved.
- [ ] c. Brunelleschi had seen *Raiders of the Lost Ark.*
- [ ] d. it made the cathedral more stable.   _____

Conclusion

4 You can <u>not</u> conclude from this story that
- [ ] a. the cathedral is still standing today.
- [ ] b. the sun falls on the metal plate only once a year.
- [x] c. Brunelleschi grew rich from his idea.
- [ ] d. it is dangerous to build on unstable ground.   _____

Clarifying Devices

5 The writer mentions Columbus to
- [ ] a. tell of another famous Italian.
- [ ] b. make the story more exciting.
- [ ] c. point out the difference in achievements of the two men.
- [x] d. give an idea of the length of time since the event.   _____

Vocabulary in Context

6 In this passage <u>feature</u> means
- [x] a. detail.
- [ ] b. main attraction.
- [ ] c. quality.
- [ ] d. focus.   _____

Add your scores for questions 1-6. Enter the total here and on the graph on page 236.   **Total Score** [ ]

Gruesome Plants

A man-eating plant? Contrary to what you see in the movies, there is no such thing. An insect-eating plant? Yes, there are many such plants, which are as voracious in their own way as Hollywood's man-eating variety.

Many carnivorous plants, like the Venus flytrap and the bladderwort, catch their prey with sudden traplike movements. Others, like certain fungi, have nooses or flypaper-like discs. Perhaps the least dangerous looking, and yet most deadly, carnivorous plant is the pitcher plant, which never has to move to catch its prey.

The American species of pitcher plant consists of a long-stemmed flower surrounded by a slender cone of leaves in the shape of a horn or pitcher. The cone is topped by a clear protruding <u>canopy</u>. Insects are attracted to the innocent looking plant by its honeylike scent. After wandering into the cone in search of sweet nectar, the insect soon finds itself sliding slowly down the slippery surface of the chamber's inner walls. Sharp, downward pointing bristles prevent the struggling prey from moving back up the cone. If the insect tries to fly out, it usually bumps into the transparent canopy and tumbles back into the trap. Waiting for the doomed insect at the bottom of the cone is a pool of fluid which contains a narcotic drug. After it has been immobilized by the drug, the insect drowns and is digested by the bacteria in the fluid. The pitcher plant then absorbs the vital nutrients.

Main Idea	1		Answer	Score
	Mark the *main idea* ⟶	**M**		15
	Mark the statement that is *too broad* ⟶	**B**		5
	Mark the statement that is *too narrow* ⟶	**N**		5
	a. The pitcher plant is a variety of carnivorous plant.	M		____
	b. There are many types of carnivorous plants.	B		____
	c. The cone of the pitcher plant is constructed to trap insects.	N		____

Score 15 points for each correct answer.   **Score**

Subject Matter

2 Another good title for this passage would be
- ☐ a. Man-eating Plants.
- ☐ b. The Carnivorous Bladderwort.
- ☐ c. The Death of an Insect.
- ☒ d. The Deadly Lure of the Pitcher Plant.   _____

Supporting Details

3 What is mentioned as the reason that insects usually can't fly out of the pitcher plant's cone?
- ☐ a. The sides of the cone are slippery.
- ☐ b. Their wings stick to the cone.
- ☐ c. The top of the cone closes over them.
- ☒ d. They hit the overhanging canopy.   _____

Conclusion

4 The passage implies that
- ☐ a. insects aren't very observant.
- ☐ b. insects would rather drink nectar than live.
- ☒ c. many insects are eaten by pitcher plants.
- ☐ d. insects learn to avoid pitcher plants.   _____

Clarifying Devices

5 The phrase "as voracious in their own way" implies that carnivorous plants
- ☐ a. eat as much as Hollywood man-eating plants.
- ☐ b. are greedier for food than man-eating plants.
- ☒ c. for their size are as greedy for food as Hollywood man-eating plants.
- ☐ d. are greedy for food, but don't really exist.   _____

Vocabulary in Context

6 The best definition for the word <u>canopy</u> is
- ☒ a. an overhanging covering.
- ☐ b. a narrow leaf.
- ☐ c. a carnivorous plant.
- ☐ d. the side of a cone.   _____

Add your scores for questions 1–6. Enter the total here and on the graph on page 236.   **Total Score** ☐

23

The Last Soldier

Yokoi Shoichi, a Japanese soldier during World War II, never surrendered. For twenty-seven years he hid deep in the jungles of Guam, a Pacific island battle site during the war. Shoichi stayed there, away from friends and foes alike, because he felt "shame and dishonor" after the war.

Shoichi knew that Japan had lost the war, but the humiliation of defeat kept him from giving himself up. So he stayed in the jungle, living on what he could scavenge. He ate mostly insects, snails, frogs and rats.

In 1972, U.S. authorities finally convinced Shoichi to "surrender." He was sent back to his homeland, Japan. Doctors who examined him there found him to be in good health, with just a touch of anemia due to a lack of iron in his diet.

Shoichi's return home attracted a lot of attention. When a department store in Tokyo exhibited his jungle clothes and tools, more than 350,000 curious people came to view them.

After spending some time back in civilization, Shoichi met a forty-five-year-old widow. The old soldier and the widow fell in love and married. After their wedding, the couple took a honeymoon trip to— of all places—the island of Guam.

Main Idea	1		Answer	Score
	Mark the *main idea* ⟶		M	15
	Mark the statement that is *too broad* ⟶		B	5
	Mark the statement that is *too narrow* ⟶		N	5

a. A soldier who refused to surrender returned to civilization after twenty-seven years. `M` _____

b. It is often difficult for soldiers to face their country's defeat. `B` _____

c. Shoichi went into hiding on Guam at the end of World War II. `N` _____

Subject Matter   **2**   The passage is mostly about

☐ a. the island of Guam.

☐ b. Yokoi Shoichi's marriage.

☐ c. the battles on Guam during World War II.

☒ d. a Japanese soldier who hid on Guam.   _____

Supporting Details   **3**   After Shoichi's return, 350,000 people in Japan

☐ a. met Yokoi Shoichi when he arrived.

☐ b. bought Yokoi Shoichi's book.

☐ c. attended Yokoi Shoichi's wedding.

☒ d. saw a display of Shoichi's clothing and equipment.   _____

Conclusion   **4**   The passage implies that Shoichi's state of good health upon returning to Japan was surprising because he had

☐ a. been exposed to harsh water.

☒ b. eaten only the food he could find in the jungle.

☐ c. gone for long periods without food.

☐ d. no medical attention for twenty-seven years.   _____

Clarifying Devices   **5**   The writer mentions Shoichi's honeymoon trip to Guam

☐ a. to show that Shoichi did not change much when he returned to civilization.

☐ b. to indicate that Shoichi had not adjusted to civilization.

☒ c. because it seems surprising that he would have wanted to return there.

☐ d. to illustrate his wife's influence.   _____

Vocabulary in Context   **6**   In this passage the word <u>scavenge</u> means to

☐ a. chew and swallow.

☐ b. catch and kill.

☒ c. search out.

☐ d. break open.   _____

Add your scores for questions 1-6. Enter the total here and on the graph on page 236.   **Total Score** ☐

24

Bird or Mammal?

Classifying animals is not always a simple process. For instance, since its discovery in the eighteenth century, the platypus has been a major problem for biologists and zoologists. This odd looking creature seems to be part mammal and part bird.

The furry platypus, a native of Australia and Tasmania, looks like a mammal at first glance. But upon looking more closely, one recognizes the birdlike characteristics which have puzzled scientists. For instance, the platypus has webbed feet like some water birds. It also has a leathery bill like a duck. That's how the animal gets its name the "duck-billed platypus." Also, the semi-aquatic platypus lays eggs like a bird.

But once the eggs are hatched, the mother nurses her young, which is typical of a mammal, not a bird. The platypus has no nipples, however, so the milk is secreted through tiny openings in the mother's stomach, and the baby laps it up. And even though the platypus has those birdlike webbed feet, at the end of the webs are claws like those of a cat or raccoon.

After much debate, scientists have finally decided to call the platypus a mammal, just to give it a classification. But it's really in a class by itself.

Main Idea	1		Answer	Score
	Mark the *main idea* ⟶	M	15
	Mark the statement that is *too broad* ⟶	B	5
	Mark the statement that is *too narrow* ⟶	N	5

a. The platypus has many birdlike characteristics. [N] _____

b. Because it has mixed characteristics, the platypus is a difficult animal to classify. [B] _____

c. Classifying certain animals is neither a simple matter, nor a precise science. [M] _____

Score 15 points for each correct answer.   **Score**

Subject Matter

2 The passage is mostly about
- ☐ a. animal classification.
- ☐ b. the breeding season of the platypus.
- ☑ c. classifying the platypus.
- ☐ d. the difficulty of classifying animals.   _____

Supporting Details

3 The platypus is most like a mammal because
- ☐ a. the female lays eggs.
- ☐ b. it has webbed feet.
- ☐ c. it is semi-aquatic.
- ☑ d. the female nurses its young.   _____

Conclusion

4 The difficulty of classifying the platypus suggests that
- ☑ a. classification of animals is not always an exact science.
- ☐ b. only the platypus has characteristics of more than one type of animal.
- ☐ c. most animals have the characteristics of more than one animal type.
- ☐ d. scientists sometimes mistakenly classify animals.   _____

Clarifying Devices

5 The writer develops the main idea by depending <u>mostly</u> on
- ☐ a. vivid adjectives and adverbs.
- ☐ b. logical reasoning.
- ☐ c. an emotional appeal.
- ☑ d. a series of examples.   _____

Vocabulary in Context

6 The best definition for <u>semi-aquatic</u> is an animal which lives
- ☐ a. in water or marshes.
- ☐ b. half under water.
- ☑ c. both in water and on land.
- ☐ d. near the edge of a lake.   _____

Add your scores for questions 1–6. Enter the total here and on the graph on page 236.   **Total Score** ☐

25

King Tut's Tomb

Thousands of years ago, Egyptian rulers, or pharaohs, were buried with great ceremony and lavish treasures that were to be used in the other world. Unfortunately, until 1922, no remains of any of the pharaohs or their treasures had ever been found. In that year, however, an archaeologist named Howard Carter and his sponsor, Lord Carnavon, were at last successful. They found the tomb of King Tutankhamen, who was buried 3,200 years ago. King Tut's tomb was the first fully preserved tomb to be uncovered in Egypt's Valley of the Kings. The two men found the tomb to contain wonderful treasures. Gold figures and magnificent furniture decorated with gold were found in the <u>myriad</u> of secret rooms and tunnels within the pyramid.

The only disappointment for Howard Carter came when he found that King Tut's body was nothing but dust. Apparently a mistake had been made when the king's body was mummified. Carter did, however, find 143 pieces of jewelry within the mummy case. These, too, were made of gold and precious stones.

Actually, despite all the publicity about King Tut, his rule as king was short and relatively uneventful. He died when he was just eighteen years old.

There is an interesting story that goes along with King Tut's tomb. People say that a powerful curse was placed in the tomb. This curse would descend on anyone uncovering King Tut's tomb. Not very long after the discovery, Lord Carnavon, along with several of the workmen died suddenly.

Main Idea	1		Answer	Score
	Mark the *main idea* $\longrightarrow$		M	15
	Mark the statement that is *too broad* $\longrightarrow$		B	5
	Mark the statement that is *too narrow* $\longrightarrow$		N	5
	a.	The tombs of Egyptian pharaohs contain great treasures.	B	
	b.	King Tut's body had not been properly mummified.	N	
	c.	King Tut's tomb, which was the first pharaoh's tomb to be uncovered, contained many treasures.	M	

Score 15 points for each correct answer.   **Score**

Subject Matter

2 The subject of this passage is
- [ ] a. the Valley of the Kings.
- [x] b. the discovery of King Tut's tomb.
- [ ] c. King Tut's accomplishments.
- [ ] d. Howard Carter, archaeologist. _____

Supporting Details

3 King Tut's body was not recovered because
- [x] a. his embalmers had made a mistake.
- [ ] b. the Egyptian government would not allow it.
- [ ] c. it had been placed in another tomb.
- [ ] d. the mummified remains were almost 3,200 years old. _____

Conclusion

4 It is apparent that King Tut
- [ ] a. was a great military leader.
- [x] b. thought a great deal of himself.
- [ ] c. was afraid of dying.
- [ ] d. was loved by the Egyptian people. _____

Clarifying Devices

5 The word *despite* serves to show a
- [ ] a. surprise.
- [ ] b. similarity.
- [x] c. contrast.
- [ ] d. correction. _____

Vocabulary in Context

6 If you have a myriad of something, you have
- [x] a. many.
- [ ] b. some.
- [ ] c. few.
- [ ] d. several. _____

Add your scores for questions 1-6. Enter the total here and on the graph on page 236.   **Total Score** ☐

26

The Deadly Moray Eel

The fearsome teeth of the moray eel are only used on human divers by accident or in self-defense. Their true purpose is to help the eel kill and eat octopi, its most common prey.

The octopi, since they have no skeletons, can slither into narrow cracks and crevices to hide from their predators. But the moray eel is also long and thin, and can easily follow an octopus into its lair. Once a moray has found an octopus, it either swallows it whole or, with larger octopi, twists the tentacles off one at a time and devours them.

The octopus has few defenses: its horny beak is no match for the moray's needle-sharp teeth, and the slippery eel just slides through the clutching tentacles. But if the octopus can escape with only one or two tentacles missing, it can grow them back. It can also use chemical warfare to hide from its enemy. A frightened octopus can produce a cloud of black ink that appears to deaden the moray eel's sense of smell. Since these eels hunt largely by smell, an eel caught by the ink cloud may actually touch the octopus without recognizing it as prey. But the octopus's best hope for survival is to avoid being found at all. So, it is no wonder that human divers find them to be shy and secretive creatures.

Main Idea	1		Answer	Score
	Mark the *main idea*	→	M	15
	Mark the statement that is *too broad*	→	B	5
	Mark the statement that is *too narrow*	→	N	5

a. The moray eel is a fearsome predator of the ocean. | B | _____

b. Moray eels have sharp teeth. | N | _____

c. The moray eel's most common prey is the octopus. | M | _____

Subject Matter

2 This passage is mostly about

☐ a. the life of an octopus.

☒ b. the moray eel and its prey.

☐ c. skin-diving adventures.

☐ d. chemical warfare in the ocean.   _____

Supporting Details

3 The cloud of black ink affects the predator by

☐ a. killing it.

☐ b. frightening it.

☐ c. angering it.

☒ d. numbing its sense of smell.   _____

Conclusion

4 Readers are likely to sympathize with the octopi because of these creatures'

☐ a. fearlessness.

☒ b. defenselessness.

☐ c. seriousness.

☐ d. carelessness.   _____

Clarifying Devices

5 The writer creates interest in the first sentence by using

☐ a. a comparison.

☒ b. an interesting fact.

☐ c. a precise argument.

☐ d. an analogy.   _____

Vocabulary in Context

6 Lair means

☒ a. resting place.

☐ b. prey.

☐ c. cave.

☐ d. shell.   _____

Add your scores for questions 1–6. Enter the total here and on the graph on page 236.   **Total Score** ☐

27

A Fifty-Year Wait

In 1924, Nordic ski events were held at the first Winter Olympics in Chamonix, France. But the American skiers came home without medals. Norway took most of the medals for cross-country and ski jumping events that year. They did the same for many years after. From 1924 through 1972, the American skiers had no medals to show for their Olympic trips. The U.S. was generally thought to be weak in ski competition.

But in 1974 it was discovered that the U.S. record was slightly better than people had been led to believe. And Norway's record was not quite as good. The discovery was a surprise and a delight to American ski fans, but even more so to American skier Anders Haugen. After fifty years, Anders got the medal he should have won back in 1924.

In the ski jump event at Chamonix in 1924, Haugen had scored in fourth place. He had just missed earning a medal. His score was 17.916, just slightly behind Thorleif Haug of Norway. Haug's score of 18 had won him the bronze medal.

But in 1974, Norway's National Olympic Committee did a check of all final Olympic results. There had been an error in <u>computing</u> Haug's score! So Haugen, now an elderly man, traveled across the ocean for his award. On September 12, 1974, he was given a bronze medal in a special ceremony at the Norway Ski Museum.

Main Idea	1		Answer	Score
	Mark the *main idea* ⟶		**M**	15
	Mark the statement that is *too broad* ⟶		**B**	5
	Mark the statement that is *too narrow* ⟶		**N**	5

a. An American skier finally received an Olympic medal when an error was discovered after 50 years. ⬜ M _____

b. Errors in scoring have sometimes been made at the Olympics. ⬜ B _____

c. For many years, American skiers received no Olympic medals. ⬜ N _____

Score 15 points for each correct answer.   Score

Subject Matter

2 Another good title for this passage would be

☐ a. The 1924 Olympics.

☐ b. Norway's Skiers.

☒ c. An Olympic Record Corrected.

☐ d. American Skiers in the Olympics.   _____

Supporting Details

3 From 1924–1972, U.S. skiers were considered weak in Olympic competition because they

☐ a. had won only two medals.

☒ b. had won no medals.

☐ c. had never entered jumping events.

☐ d. had won only one medal.   _____

Conclusion

4 Which of the following is most likely true?

☐ a. Norwegians are naturally better skiers than Americans.

☐ b. The U.S. ski team can never win as many Olympic medals as Norway.

☒ c. When the Winter Olympics began, the Norwegians had more experience and training than the Americans.

☐ d. In time, the American Olympic skiers will definitely be better than the Norwegians.   _____

Clarifying Devices

5 The writer says "the discovery was a surprise and a delight to American ski fans" in order to

☒ a. show that the error and its correction were important to ski fans as well as to Haugen.

☐ b. show that the error was more important to fans than to Haugen.

☐ c. suggest that the Americans cared more about the error than the Norwegians.

☐ d. suggest that there had been no error.   _____

Vocabulary in Context

6 The best definition for the word <u>computing</u> is

☐ a. writing.

☐ b. judging.

☒ c. figuring.

☐ d. multiplying.   _____

Add your scores for questions 1–6. Enter the total here and on the graph on page 236.   Total Score ☐

28

The Story of Storks

The story that babies are brought into the home by the stork may have started in northwestern Europe, where the stork is a commonplace sight and is well respected. The stork has white feathers, black wing quills and a red beak and legs. It stalks fish and other small water creatures in meadows and marshes, and is sometimes seen in high places such as steeples or chimneys, standing on one leg.

The stork has often been regarded as a sign of good luck. Whenever a pair of storks built a nest on a housetop, the Romans regarded it as a sign of good fortune from Venus, the goddess of love. The stork was also the good luck bird in Germany and the Netherlands. These superstitions persist today. In some places, wheels are put on the tops of houses to give storks nesting places.

Centuries ago, there was already a belief that the stork flew over a house where a birth was about to take place, bringing good luck to the family. The story of storks delivering babies probably arose from this superstition and from many fathers' and mothers' difficulty in explaining to their other children where the new baby came from. It is quite understandable that they should use the symbol of good luck and the guardian of the home to help explain the arrival of a new member of the family.

Main Idea	1		Answer	Score
	Mark the *main idea* ⟶	M		15
	Mark the statement that is *too broad* ⟶	B		5
	Mark the statement that is *too narrow* ⟶	N		5
	a. Storks have long been regarded as signs of good luck.	M		
	b. There have been many fables about storks.	B		
	c. The stork is said to deliver new babies.	N		

Score 15 points for each correct answer.   **Score**

Subject Matter

2 The subject matter of this passage is
- ☐ a. ancient fables.
- ☐ b. good luck signs.
- ☐ c. nursery rhymes about the stork.
- ☒ d. legends about the stork.   _____

Supporting Details

3 The Romans thought storks were
- ☐ a. rather ungainly birds.
- ☒ b. signs of good fortune.
- ☐ c. responsible for babies.
- ☐ d. only good for eating.   _____

Conclusion

4 The passage suggests that the story of the stork delivering babies
- ☐ a. was extremely harmful to children.
- ☐ b. was an understandable fantasy at the time it was used.
- ☐ c. may have been true.
- ☒ d. was confusing to many people.   _____

Clarifying Devices

5 This passage can best be described as a
- ☐ a. myth.
- ☐ b. descriptive essay.
- ☐ c. joke.
- ☒ d. story.   _____

Vocabulary in Context

6 In this passage symbol means
- ☐ a. a loud instrument.
- ☒ b. something that stands for an idea.
- ☐ c. a letter or number.
- ☐ d. an emblem.   _____

Add your scores for questions 1-6. Enter the total here and on the graph on page 236.

Total Score ☐

29

Kissing Under the Mistletoe

During the Christmas season, many people keep alive the romantic custom of kissing under a sprig of the "vampire plant." The "vampire plant"? That's right. This is a little-known but <u>apt</u> nickname for the common mistletoe plant. In the wild, the mistletoe feeds greedily on other plants.

Herbs and shrubs of the American species of mistletoe are parasitic. In other words, like vampires, they suck the life out of the plants on which they live. Dense bunches of mistletoe infest the branches of trees or other shrubs. Their narrow stems send out roots which invade the tissue of the host plants, robbing them of nourishment. Occasionally, a mistletoe will even attach itself to another mistletoe! If a mistletoe becomes too successful at sapping food from its host, it may kill the host and then die of starvation.

Historically, the mistletoe has been surrounded by a wealth of superstition and folklore. Although the "vampire plant" is often fatal to other plants, it was used in ancient times as a cure-all for various human ailments. The mistletoe was sacred to many early religious groups. One of these groups, the Druids of England, are believed to have originated the custom of kissing under a sprig of the plant.

Main Idea	1		Answer	Score
	Mark the *main idea*	→	M	15
	Mark the statement that is *too broad*	→	B	5
	Mark the statement that is *too narrow*	→	N	5

a. The mistletoe is a parasitic plant that has been surrounded by much superstition and folklore. 〔M〕 _____

b. The mistletoe drains the life out of its host plant. 〔N〕 _____

c. There are many stories associated with the mistletoe. 〔B〕 _____

Score 15 points for each correct answer.   **Score**

Subject Matter

2 The passage deals mostly with

☐ a. kissing under the mistletoe.

☒ b. mistletoe in the wild.

☐ c. parasitic plants.

☐ d. the Druids' use of the mistletoe.   _____

Supporting Details

3 The mistletoe saps nutrients by

☐ a. strangling its host.

☐ b. tapping into its host's roots.

☒ c. sending roots into its host's tissue.

☐ d. covering its host.   _____

Conclusion

4 The passage implies that the mistletoe

☒ a. is a menace to other plants.

☐ b. is helpful to other plants.

☐ c. may be harmful to humans.

☐ d. always kills its host.   _____

Clarifying Devices

5 The first sentence of the passage catches the reader's interest by

☐ a. talking about the Christmas season.

☒ b. contrasting a romantic custom with the mistletoe's monstrous nickname.

☐ c. suggesting that kissing can be very dangerous.

☐ d. talking about a romantic custom.   _____

Vocabulary in Context

6 <u>Apt</u> means

☐ a. strange.

☐ b. old.

☒ c. fitting.

☐ d. inappropriate.   _____

Add your scores for questions 1-6. Enter the total here and on the graph on page 236.   **Total Score** ☐

30

Are You a Good Detective?

Would you like to spend an evening reading a lovely story with beautiful illustrations and make $35,000 at the same time? Millions of people all over the world tried to do just that. Only one succeeded. The book is called *Masquerade*, and was written by British painter Kit Williams. Within its pages are clues to the location of a golden jewel, and whoever figured out the clues could find and keep the treasure.

Some years ago, Williams was asked to write a children's book. Wanting to do something no one else had done before, he decided to bury a golden treasure and tell where it was in the book. He began painting without a clear idea of what the story would be about, where he would bury the treasure, or even what the treasure would be. As he painted, he decided that in the story a hare, or rabbit, would travel through earth, air, fire and water to deliver a gift from the moon to the sun.

After three years, he finished the paintings and then wrote the story. The treasure became an 18-carat gold hare, adorned with <u>precious</u> stones, and it was made by Kit Williams himself. This beautiful jewel, worth around $35,000, depending on gold prices, was buried somewhere in Britain, free to anyone who could decipher the clues. Williams's assurance that a ten year old was as likely to find it as a college graduate helped the book sell millions of copies and kept people of all ages amused trying to solve the mystery of *Masquerade*.

The rabbit was finally found in the spring of 1982, by a 48-year-old design engineer. It was buried in a park about thirty-five miles from London.

Main Idea	1		Answer	Score
	Mark the *main idea* ⟶	M		15
	Mark the statement that is *too broad* ⟶	B		5
	Mark the statement that is *too narrow* ⟶	N		5

a. The clues in *Masquerade* led the reader to the site of buried treasure.   M   N ☐ _____

b. *Masquerade* tells a story of a hare's adventure.   N ☐ _____

c. Some books lead people on wonderful adventures.   B ☐ _____

Score 15 points for each correct answer.   **Score**

Subject Matter

2 Another good title for this passage would be

☐ a. British Painters.
☐ b. Golden Jewelry.
☒ c. A Modern Treasure Hunt.
☐ d. Writing Children's Books. _____

Supporting Details

3 When Williams began working on his book, he

☐ a. was paid $35,000.
☐ b. learned to paint.
☐ c. had already buried the treasure.
☒ d. did not know what the story would be about. _____

Conclusion

4 We can conclude from the passage that

☐ a. the clues in *Masquerade* are easy to decipher.
☒ b. Kit Williams has many artistic talents.
☐ c. many people bury treasures in Britain.
☐ d. Kit Williams said he would pay $35,000 to whoever found the treasure. _____

Clarifying Devices

5 The function of the first sentence in this passage is to

☐ a. give detail.
☐ b. sum up the story.
☒ c. capture the reader's interest.
☐ d. elaborate upon a point. _____

Vocabulary in Context

6 The best meaning for <u>precious</u> in this passage is

☒ a. valuable.
☐ b. beloved.
☐ c. elegant.
☐ d. cute. _____

Add your scores for questions 1–6. Enter the total here and on the graph on page 236.

Total Score ☐

31

The Graveyard of Elephants

Fortune hunters used to think that if they could find the elephants' graveyard they would be rich. Legend had it that old elephants, when they knew they were near death, would all go to the same secret spot in the jungle to die. According to some accounts, an animal that was wounded or sick would be guided and half carried by other elephants so that it could reach this sacred spot. Of course, if this were true, it would mean that a fortune in ivory would have accumulated at this hidden place. However, despite numerous attempts, no one has found this mysterious graveyard.

Recently, however, people have become more interested in learning about live elephants than in developing <u>schemes</u> for finding the tusks of dead ones. Interested scientists who have journeyed to Africa have watched elephants in the wild for years, allowing the elephants to get used to them so they could observe their behavior at close range. What they have learned about elephants is far more exciting than the location of some secret burial site. Researchers have found that elephants are very intelligent and social animals that form strong friendships among themselves and help to defend and raise each other's calves. The sympathetic elephants that crowd around one of their wounded friends are actually trying to nurse and protect it, not lead it off to some mythical graveyard.

Main Idea 1

	Answer	Score
Mark the *main idea* ⟶	M	15
Mark the statement that is *too broad* ⟶	B	5
Mark the statement that is *too narrow* ⟶	N	5

a. Today, people are more interested in learning about live elephants than in finding the mythical elephant graveyard. M ____

b. Fortune hunters, hearing the legend, have tried to find the elephants' graveyard. N ____

c. There are many false legends about animals. B ____

Score 15 points for each correct answer.   **Score**

Subject Matter

2 This passage focuses mostly on

- ☐ a. fortune hunters.
- ☐ b. elephant legends.
- ☒ c. facts about elephants.
- ☐ d. dead elephants.

_____

Supporting Details

3 According to legends about the elephant graveyard

- ☐ a. elephants lived there from time to time.
- ☐ b. elephants were not the only animals who went there.
- ☒ c. other elephants helped to carry wounded elephants to the graveyard.
- ☐ d. the graveyard was once a well-known spot.

_____

Conclusion

4 From this passage, we can infer that the writer

- ☐ a. is disappointed that the legend is not true.
- ☐ b. thinks that elephants are cute and cuddly.
- ☐ c. is scornful of people who believe in the elephant graveyard.
- ☒ d. thinks live elephants are much more interesting than dead ones.

_____

Clarifying Devices

5 The writer contrasts the behavior of fortune hunters with

- ☐ a. live elephants.
- ☒ b. those who are truly interested in elephants.
- ☐ c. other jungle adventurers.
- ☐ d. elephant hunters.

_____

Vocabulary in Context

6 The best substitute for the word <u>schemes</u> in this passage would be

- ☒ a. plans.
- ☐ b. expeditions.
- ☐ c. trails.
- ☐ d. stories.

_____

Add your scores for questions 1–6. Enter the total here and on the graph on page 236.

Total Score ☐

32

A Strange Naval Battle

Arahwe was a strange name for a battleship, but the name was fitting, for the *Arahwe* was a strange battleship. The ship was the only American naval vessel that fought its only battle on dry land. The *Arahwe* was built in the 1860s, but never saw action until many years later, when it was traveling along the coast of Chile.

The *Arahwe*'s adventure began one day when a massive underwater earthquake occurred right off the coast of Chile. Gigantic waves heaved the ship up on dry land. It was grounded along with several other boats. The *Arahwe* looked helpless and was tempting bait for looters who came on the scene to plunder the shipwrecked boats. When the robbers tried to climb aboard the ship, the crew beat them off with much difficulty. When the looters banded together again for an all-out assault on the ship, the crew knew they were in trouble.

Captain Alexander of the *Arahwe* ordered the gun crew to load the cannon. However, the sailors were unable to reach the cannonballs, which were stored below in the twisted wreckage. Faced with this dilemma, the Captain thought of a substitute for the cannonballs. He ordered the sailors to bring up a basket of hard round cheeses from the kitchen.

When the mob charged at the ship, Captain Alexander ordered the cannons to be fired. Balls of cheese knocked over some of the bandits. When another round of cheese was fired, the mob retreated wildly. After this victory, the *Arahwe* was safe, but it never made it back to sea. It is gallantly listed in the Navy's records as "lost in action."

Main Idea	1		Answer	Score
	Mark the *main idea*	→	M	15
	Mark the statement that is *too broad*	→	B	5
	Mark the statement that is *too narrow*	→	N	5
	a. The *Arahwe* fought an unusual battle.		B	___
	b. The *Arahwe* fought its only battle on land, by firing cheese from cannons.		M	___
	c. The *Arahwe* was involved in a battle on land.		N	___

Score 15 points for each correct answer.   **Score**

Subject   **2** This passage is primarily about
Matter
- [ ] a. Chile.
- [x] b. the *Arahwe*.
- [ ] c. Captain Alexander.
- [ ] d. balls of cheese.   _____

Supporting **3** The *Arahwe* was grounded in
Details
- [ ] a. Cuba.
- [ ] b. Florida.
- [x] c. Chile.
- [ ] d. Brazil.   _____

Conclusion **4** Using cheese instead of cannonballs was
- [ ] a. expensive.
- [x] b. effective.
- [ ] c. sinful.
- [ ] d. wasteful.   _____

Clarifying **5** The writer creates interest in the first sentence by
Devices
- [ ] a. telling a joke.
- [ ] b. describing the ship.
- [ ] c. reading from the ship's log.
- [x] d. talking about the ship's strange name.   _____

Vocabulary **6** The word <u>dilemma,</u> as used in the passage,
in Context   means
- [x] a. problem.
- [ ] b. puzzle.
- [ ] c. mystery.
- [ ] d. crime.   _____

Add your scores for questions 1-6. Enter the   Total
total here and on the graph on page 236.   Score [   ]

33

Mount Trashmore

The newest mountain in the world is located near Virginia Beach, Virginia, and is made completely of trash. When the city had problems finding ways to dispose of its garbage, it decided to turn a swampy, fifty-acre trash dump into a mountainous disposal area. The plan called for the creation of recreation areas when the mountain was finished. The mountain would have bicycle trails, tennis courts and two man-made lakes.

To begin with, the city <u>drained</u> the swampy area and built a road to the site. Then trash was collected and spread over the land. The trash was covered with a layer of soil, and heavy mechanical compactors rolled over everything, crushing the trash. New layers of trash and dirt were added and crushed over and over again until there was a huge mound, sixty-five feet high, made of 640,000 tons of trash. Finally, bull-dozers dug out two lakes near the bottom of the mountain, and grass was planted on the top layer of dirt. The lakes provide fishing and boating for local residents.

Building trash mountains is a new solution to the problems of garbage disposal. The mountains can also provide recreation areas for the people who live near them. Many people now enjoy sledding and skiing on the slopes of Mount Trashmore.

Main Idea 1

	Answer	Score
Mark the *main idea* ⟶	M	15
Mark the statement that is *too broad* ⟶	B	5
Mark the statement that is *too narrow* ⟶	N	5
a. Mountains can be made of anything.	B	___
b. Man-made lakes on Mount Trashmore provide fishing and boating.	N	___
c. A trash mountain is a good new solution to the problem of trash disposal.	M	___

Score 15 points for each correct answer.   **Score**

Subject Matter

2 The best alternate title for this passage would be

- ☐ a. Trash Disposal Methods.
- ☐ b. Fun with Garbage.
- ☑ c. Building a Mountain.
- ☐ d. Trashy Building.   _____

Supporting Details

3 Plans for the mountain did <u>not</u> include a

- ☐ a. ski area.
- ☐ b. lake for fishing.
- ☑ c. basketball court.
- ☐ d. bicycle trail.   _____

Conclusion

4 This passage implies that

- ☐ a. people enjoy walking through trash.
- ☐ b. new mountains are all made of garbage.
- ☑ c. this method of trash disposal can be used by other communities.
- ☐ d. burying trash isn't a good idea.   _____

Clarifying Devices

5 The writer demonstrates the practical uses of such a mountain by

- ☐ a. outlining the process of building a mountain.
- ☐ b. describing advantages of mountains.
- ☑ c. giving examples of its recreational uses.
- ☐ d. telling the opinions of the local residents.   _____

Vocabulary in Context

6 The swamp was <u>drained</u>, which means

- ☐ a. it was all used up.
- ☐ b. the water evaporated from it.
- ☑ c. the water was pumped out of it.
- ☐ d. the land was dug up.   _____

Add your scores for questions 1–6. Enter the total here and on the graph on page 236.   **Total Score** ☐

34

What's It Like Outside?

Since ancient times, the complicated patterns and unpredictable turns of the weather have confused forecasters. Today, <u>meteorologists</u> can explain much of what has already happened with the weather, but little of what will happen in the future.

The Chinese have found a way to predict the weather that may be superior to all modern techniques—listening to the croak of a frog! This method has been proven accurate 80 percent of the time. The formula for forecasting is quite simple: if frogs croak on a fine day, it will rain in two days; if frogs croak after rain, there will be fine weather; it will continue to rain if frogs do not croak after successive days.

Crickets have been proven to be good thermometers in warm weather. By counting the number of cricket chirps in fifteen seconds, and adding thirty-seven to the number, you will arrive at the temperature, within a few degrees Fahrenheit.

Surprising as it may seem, scientists have determined that we are in the middle of an ice age. Since 1945, the earth has once more begun to cool down. The warm period right now is just a phase of the ice age. It is known as the "interglacial period."

Main Idea	1		Answer	Score
	Mark the *main idea* →		M	15
	Mark the statement that is *too broad* →		B	5
	Mark the statement that is *too narrow* →		N	5

a. All weather forecasters grow frustrated trying to predict the weather. [B] _____

b. Predicting the weather has always been a difficult task. [M] _____

c. The Chinese have found a way to predict the weather by using frogs. [N] _____

Subject Matter   **2**   This passage is about

- ☐ a. glaciers.
- ☒ b. weather.
- ☐ c. frogs.
- ☐ d. meteorologists.   ————

Supporting Details   **3**   When frogs croak on a nice day, it means

- ☐ a. the weather will be fair for a week.
- ☐ b. rain will fall within the day.
- ☐ c. the weather is getting worse.
- ☒ d. rain is two days away.   ————

Conclusion   **4**   According to the passage, in cold weather, crickets probably don't

- ☒ a. chirp.
- ☐ b. count.
- ☐ c. predict the weather.
- ☐ d. eat.   ————

Clarifying Devices   **5**   An interglacial period is a period

- ☐ a. of perfect weather conditions.
- ☐ b. after two glacial periods.
- ☒ c. between two glacial periods.
- ☐ d. before two glacial periods.   ————

Vocabulary in Context   **6**   Meteorologists have skill in

- ☐ a. tracking meteors.
- ☒ b. weather forecasting.
- ☐ c. repairing weather stations.
- ☐ d. counting cricket chirps.   ————

Add your scores for questions 1-6. Enter the total here and on the graph on page 236.   **Total Score** ☐

35

The World of Gambling

Some people do it for fun and excitement. Some do it in hope of making a profit. Others have become so adept at it that one might call them "professionals." And, there are even a few unfortunates who are hopelessly addicted to it.

Whatever the motivation, gambling attracts millions of players each year to race tracks, gaming tables and slot machines. The prospect of turning a few dollars into hundreds or even thousands of dollars has intrigued gamblers of all abilities and temperaments.

Some gamblers are good or even brilliant at gambling, but don't realize they have a special talent until it is too late. This was the case with a young sailor who visited the casinos of Las Vegas in 1950. The young man stood at the craps table and made an unbelievable twenty-seven passes, or wins, in a row. It had never been done before. Unfortunately for the stunned sailor, his amazing luck with the dice was not matched by very spectacular wagering. His legendary feat garnered him only $750.

Compulsive gamblers are gamblers who lose and lose but cannot stop gambling. These victims of gambling fever are little better off than if they had a real physical sickness.

In the state of Nevada, where the city of Las Vegas is located, most people find the time and the money to do some gambling. On the average, residents of Nevada wager about $850 a year.

Main Idea 1

	Answer	Score
Mark the *main idea* ⟶	M	15
Mark the statement that is *too broad* ⟶	B	5
Mark the statement that is *too narrow* ⟶	N	5

a. Gambling is one way in which people amuse themselves. `B` ____

b. Some people have a special talent for gambling. `N` ____

c. There are many ways to gamble and many kinds of gamblers. `M` ____

Subject
Matter

2 The subject of this passage is

- [ ] a. poker playing.
- [x] b. gambling.
- [ ] c. casinos.
- [ ] d. Las Vegas.   _____

Supporting
Details

3 As the writer mentions, for some unfortunate people, gambling can be

- [ ] a. fun.
- [x] b. addictive.
- [ ] c. frightening.
- [ ] d. dangerous.   _____

Conclusion

4 Most likely, the state which harbors the most gamblers is

- [ ] a. Texas.
- [ ] b. New York.
- [x] c. New Jersey.
- [ ] d. Nevada.   _____

Clarifying
Devices

5 In the opening paragraph, the writer

- [x] a. attempts to spark the reader's curiosity.
- [ ] b. forgets to mention the subject of the passage.
- [ ] c. tries to confuse the reader.
- [ ] d. says exactly what the passage is going to be about.   _____

Vocabulary
in Context

6 A person who is <u>compulsive</u> is

- [ ] a. skillful at a job.
- [ ] b. incapable of anything.
- [x] c. driven by an irresistible urge.
- [ ] d. serious most of the time.   _____

Add your scores for questions 1–6. Enter the
total here and on the graph on page 236.

Total
Score [ ]

36

Great Eating

Many people would rate the lobster as one of the most delicious of all seafoods, and it can claim several other titles as well. The American species is the heaviest, longest-lived, and fastest-moving of all crustaceans.

Lobsters continue to grow for as long as they live, which may be for fifty years or so. The oldest lobsters are a far cry in size from the young three-pounders that grace dinner tables. A twenty-three-pound lobster caught in Maine in 1891 had a crushing claw alone that was fourteen inches long. Six years later, a lobster that weighed thirty-four pounds and was almost two feet long from nose to tail tip was caught off the New Jersey coast. But the record is held by a whopper, picked up in 600 feet of water off the Virginia shoreline in 1934, that weighed in at forty-two pounds, seven ounces.

It is unlikely that many more monster lobsters will ever be found; they are too popular on the dinner table, and are hunted so heavily that none could escape for the forty or fifty years needed to grow to record size. The lobster can travel quickly, shooting backwards with a powerful flip of its tail, but its speed is no help in escaping its human predators, who lure lobsters into traps with bits of well-rotted fish as bait.

Main Idea 1		Answer	Score
Mark the *main idea*	→	M	15
Mark the statement that is *too broad*	→	B	5
Mark the statement that is *too narrow*	→	N	5

a. The lobster grows as long as it is alive. | N | _____

b. The lobster is a popular seafood. | B | _____

c. American lobsters are the heaviest, longest-lived and fastest crustaceans. | M | _____

Subject Matter

2 This passage deals with

☑ a. lobsters.

☐ b. seafood.

☐ c. records.

☐ d. the extinction of lobsters.   _____

Supporting Details

3 Why do lobsters get so heavy?

☒ a. They continue to grow for as long as they live.

☐ b. After they get fairly large, nothing can kill them.

☐ c. They eat a lot of shellfish.

☐ d. Survival in deep water demands that they grow large.   _____

Conclusion

4 This passage indicates that lobsters

☐ a. go on living until caught.

☐ b. of great size no longer exist.

☐ c. will lose their popularity.

☒ d. are mainly caught and killed by humans.   _____

Clarifying Devices

5 The author tells us about very large old lobsters by

☐ a. telling horror stories.

☒ b. giving measurements.

☐ c. telling of personal experiences.

☐ d. setting up contrasts.   _____

Vocabulary in Context

6 Grace, in this passage, means to

☐ a. bless.

☐ b. smooth.

☒ c. adorn.

☐ d. favor.   _____

Add your scores for questions 1–6. Enter the total here and on the graph on page 236.   **Total Score** ☐

37

An Ancient Disaster

For more than six hundred years, Pompeii was an important city in the Roman Empire. Located on the Bay of Naples in southern Italy, Pompeii was a favorite spot for wealthy Romans to build their country villas. The city was busy and prosperous, and the streets were lined with shops, houses and temples. Citizens had use of an open-air theater and public baths. But this dream city had one flaw. Pompeii sat at the foot of Mount Vesuvius.

In A.D. 79, on the morning of August 24, Vesuvius erupted violently. Fire and ash filled the sky and buried the beautiful city. When Vesuvius finally settled down, Pompeii lay buried under pumice nearly ten feet thick. The volcano so changed the area that the spot where Pompeii, a port city, once stood was now two miles from the ocean. Many people died in the great eruption, either from falling rock and collapsing buildings or from the volcano's poisonous fumes. The great city of Pompeii had disappeared.

So, it was a great surprise when, in the 1700s, a peasant discovered some statues buried in his vineyard. When people began to dig further, they unearthed the houses, food and even the bodies of some of the citizens of the once bustling Pompeii.

Main Idea	1		Answer	Score
	Mark the *main idea* ———————→		M	15
	Mark the statement that is *too broad* ———→		B	5
	Mark the statement that is *too narrow* ———→		N	5
	a. The city of Pompeii was once an important city in the Roman Empire.		N	_____
	b. The great city of Pompeii was completely destroyed and buried by a volcanic eruption.		M	_____
	c. Violent volcanic eruptions often destroy cities and kill people.		B	_____

Score 15 points for each correct answer.   **Score**

Subject Matter

2 Another good title for this selection would be
- [ ] a. Dream City.
- [x] b. The Great Buried City.
- [ ] c. A Famous Volcano.
- [ ] d. The Mischief of Vesuvius.   _____

Supporting Details

3 The city of Pompeii was a favorite spot for wealthy Romans because it was
- [ ] a. excellent for fishing.
- [x] b. located near the water.
- [ ] c. busy.
- [ ] d. lined with shops.   _____

Conclusion

4 The writer expresses amazement at the
- [ ] a. Roman Empire.
- [ ] b. popularity of Pompeii.
- [ ] c. beautiful city of Pompeii.
- [x] d. devastating work of the volcano.   _____

Clarifying Devices

5 The writer develops the main idea through the use of
- [ ] a. contrast.
- [ ] b. negative arguments.
- [x] c. vivid description.
- [x] d. reasoning.   _____

Vocabulary in Context

6 Bustling means
- [ ] a. crowded.
- [ ] b. prosperous.
- [x] c. noisy and busy.
- [ ] d. beautiful.   _____

Add your scores for questions 1–6. Enter the total here and on the graph on page 236.   **Total Score** ☐

38

The Quirks of Some Famous People

Most famous people have some quirk or unusual story associated with their names. Casanova, for example, was a legend in his own time. He was the epitome of the gallant adventurer and lover. However, he spent thirteen years of his life as a librarian! Casanova semi-retired to a quiet life in Bohemia, working as a librarian for Count von Waldstein in the Chateau de Dux.

Thomas Edison, the brilliant inventor, was deaf from the age of twelve. The young Edison's hearing loss was long believed to have been caused when he tried to catch a moving train and a conductor grabbed him by the ears to pull him on board. Edison himself liked to tell this story. No one is really sure how he did lose his hearing.

Great writers and artists often require various types of inspirational warm-up before they create. Rudyard Kipling could not write unless his pen was filled with black ink, and only black ink. Ludwig van Beethoven poured icy cold water over his head before he composed his music. He felt that the cold water would refresh his brain. The author Charles Dickens always faced north when working or sleeping. Tycho Brahe, an important Danish astronomer, had his nose shot off in a duel with a Danish nobleman in 1566. He replaced it with another nose made of gold. President James Garfield could simultaneously write Latin with one hand and Greek with the other. And Attila the Hun's mother was a three-and-a-half-foot dwarf!

Main Idea	1		Answer	Score
		Mark the *main idea* ⟶	M	15
		Mark the statement that is *too broad* ⟶	B	5
		Mark the statement that is *too narrow* ⟶	N	5
		a. Many facts about famous people are common knowledge.	B	____
		b. Composers have curious habits.	N	____
		c. Most famous people have an unusual story associated with their name.	M	____

Subject Matter	**2**	This passage is about famous

☐ a. scientists.
☒ b. personalities.
☐ c. composers.
☐ d. leaders. _____

Supporting Details **3** Tycho Brahe was an important

☐ a. Danish nobleman.
☒ b. Swedish astronomer.
☐ c. Swedish adventurer.
☐ d. Swedish composer. _____

Conclusion **4** Evidently, most artists and writers require

☒ a. inspiration.
☐ b. quiet.
☐ c. money.
☐ d. madness. _____

Clarifying Devices **5** A cliché is an overused expression. A cliché used in this passage is

☐ a. "grabbed him by the ears."
☒ b. "a legend in his own time."
☐ c. "his solution was to replace it."
☐ d. "semi-retired to a quiet life." _____

Vocabulary in Context **6** The epitome of something is the

☒ a. ideal.
☐ b. worst.
☐ c. most famous.
☐ d. opposite. _____

Add your scores for questions 1-6. Enter the total here and on the graph on page 236. **Total Score** ☐

39

A Wise Man

He was a funny looking man with a cheerful face, good-natured and a great talker. He was described by his student, the great philosopher Plato, as "the best and most just and wisest man." Yet, this same man was condemned to death for his beliefs.

The man was the Greek philosopher, Socrates, and he was condemned for not believing in the recognized gods and for corrupting young people. The second charge stemmed from his association with numerous young men who came to Athens from all over the civilized world to study under him.

Socrates' method of teaching was to ask questions and, by pretending not to know the answers, to press his students into thinking for themselves. His teachings had unsurpassed influence on all the great Greek and Roman schools of philosophy. Yet, for all his fame and influence, Socrates himself never wrote a word.

Socrates encouraged new ideas and free thinking in the young, and this was frightening to conservative Athenians. They wanted him silenced. Yet, many were probably surprised that he accepted death so readily.

Socrates had the right to ask for a lesser penalty, and he probably could have swayed enough of the slender majority which condemned him. But Socrates, as a firm believer in law, reasoned that it was proper to submit to the death sentence. So, he calmly accepted his fate and drank a cup of poison hemlock in the presence of his grief-stricken friends and students.

		Answer	Score
Main Idea 1			
	Mark the *main idea* ⟶	**M**	15
	Mark the statement that is *too broad* ⟶	**B**	5
	Mark the statement that is *too narrow* ⟶	**N**	5

a. Socrates' philosophical beliefs had a great impact on his life and on all of Greek and Roman philosophy. ⬜ M _____

b. Ancient Greek philosophers had a great influence on philosophical thought. ⬜ B _____

c. Socrates faced his trial and death sentence bravely by sticking to his firm beliefs. ⬜ N _____

Score 15 points for each correct answer. **Score**

Subject Matter

2 If you were to choose another title for the passage, the best one would be

☐ a. Socrates and Plato.
☐ b. The Trial of Socrates.
☐ c. Socrates' Influence on Philosophy.
☒ d. Socrates—A Man of Strong Beliefs. _____

Supporting Details

3 Socrates was condemned to death because he

☐ a. refused to beg for mercy.
☒ b. was convicted of corrupting the young.
☐ c. founded a school of philosophy.
☐ d. wrote articles attacking the Greek gods. _____

Conclusion

4 By mentioning that Socrates himself never wrote a word, the writer implies that

☐ a. Socrates was not as wise as he is reputed to have been.
☐ b. Socrates claimed the work of his students as his own.
☒ c. it is surprising that his fame and influence were so great.
☐ d. it is possible that Socrates never existed. _____

Clarifying Devices

5 In the first paragraph, the word "yet" indicates

☐ a. the time of an occurrence.
☐ b. a confirmation.
☒ c. a contradiction or contrast.
☐ d. that a definition will follow. _____

Vocabulary in Context

6 The word <u>unsurpassed</u> is closest in meaning to

☐ a. not important.
☒ b. not equaled.
☐ c. not noticed.
☐ d. not expected. _____

Add your scores for questions 1-6. Enter the total here and on the graph on page 236.

Total Score ☐

40

Stylish Living?

The royal palace at Versailles, the center of court life during the reign of Louis XIV, is today a symbol of dazzling beauty and opulent living. Millions of gold francs were spent in building and furnishing its lavish chambers, halls and gardens. So, it is difficult to imagine the royal palace as it was in its heyday—cold, crowded and filthy.

The chimneys in the palace were so wide that fires were easily extinguished by rain or snow, and wind blew smoke back into the chambers. Heating the enormous rooms was impossible, so ladies who wore fashionably low-cut dresses suffered for style.

Louis XIV enlarged the palace greatly, but because he preferred to have his nobles near him, the vast estate still swarmed with courtiers, sometimes as many as 10,000. He also favored giving the populace the opportunity to observe their sovereign at home. Sightseers were allowed to troop through the staterooms and gaze upon the king as he dined.

The hallways were as private as city streets. They were filled with vendors, tradesmen and beggars. Cows and goats were brought to the doors of the chambers to be milked. Because there were no bathroom facilities, animal and human filth piled up in the passageways of the palace.

So, with thousands of courtiers living closely together, with halls crowded with vendors and gawking townspeople, with courtyards filled with animals, with filth everywhere, it is hard to imagine this royal palace as a fitting place for lavish and elegant living.

Main Idea	1		Answer	Score
	Mark the *main idea*	→	M	15
	Mark the statement that is *too broad*	→	B	5
	Mark the statement that is *too narrow*	→	N	5

a. At its height, the magnificent palace of Versailles was actually an unpleasant place to live. ⬜ M _____

b. Versailles was very unsanitary due to overcrowding with people and animals. ⬜ N _____

c. Life in palaces of the past was less glorious than most people think. ⬜ B _____

Score 15 points for each correct answer.   **Score**

Subject Matter

2 The passage focuses on the
  - ☐ a. reign of Louis XIV.
  - ☐ b. construction of Versailles.
  - ☑ c. discomforts of Versailles.
  - ☐ d. beauty of Versailles.   _____

Supporting Details

3 According to the passage, Louis XIV believed in
  - ☐ a. maintaining large gardens.
  - ☐ b. keeping the palace cold.
  - ☐ c. the need for a quiet retreat.
  - ☑ d. allowing people to view their king.   _____

Conclusion

4 At Versailles, during the reign of Louis XIV, you would <u>not</u> have expected to find
  - ☐ a. fine paintings and statues.
  - ☑ b. comfortable living quarters.
  - ☐ c. government officials and nobles.
  - ☐ d. peasants and vendors.   _____

Clarifying Devices

5 In developing the main idea, the writer relies mostly on
  - ☐ a. quotations.
  - ☐ b. picturesque language.
  - ☐ c. emotion.
  - ☑ d. description.   _____

Vocabulary in Context

6 As used in the passage, <u>opulent</u> means
  - ☑ a. rich.
  - ☐ b. middle-class.
  - ☐ c. isolated.
  - ☐ d. comfortable.   _____

Add your scores for questions 1-6. Enter the total here and on the graph on page 236.   **Total Score** ☐

41

Want to Buy the Brooklyn Bridge?

As a rule, practical jokers either get stupendous laughs or get themselves into stupendous trouble. The outcome of a practical joke depends a great deal on the patience and sense of humor of the victims. Sometimes, however, a practical joke can be so <u>outrageous</u> that the only people who see the humor in it are the practical jokers themselves.

For two practical jokers named Lozier and DeVoe, the latter case was certainly true. Both gentlemen were retired and living in New York in 1824. It was not long before these two restless men were getting all the excitement they could handle.

It is a known fact that the southern portion of the island of Manhattan is sinking slowly into the ocean because of the weight of the many large buildings there. The practical joke was to convince fellow New Yorkers that the only way to save the island was to turn it around so the higher northern portion would be in the south, and the lower southern portion would be in the north.

Full-page ads were placed in newspapers to recruit an army of construction workers. The ad also mentioned that a gigantic anchor had been ordered and was now available, to keep the island from blowing out to sea during a storm once the island had been twisted around.

On the appointed day, hundreds of workers appeared for their first day of work. Fortunately for the practical jokers, they were nowhere to be found. Rumor had it that a sudden illness had sent Lozier and DeVoe on an indefinitely long trip to an unknown destination.

Main Idea	1		Answer	Score
	Mark the *main idea* —————→		M	15
	Mark the statement that is *too broad* ———→		B	5
	Mark the statement that is *too narrow* ———→		N	5

a. Lozier and DeVoe convinced hundreds of New Yorkers that they should turn Manhattan around. ☐ _____

b. Practical jokes can fool many people. ☐ _____

c. The southern end of the island of Manhattan is sinking. ☐ _____

Score 15 points for each correct answer. **Score**

Subject Matter **2** The subject of this passage is
- ☐ a. the island of Manhattan.
- ☐ b. the life of Lozier and DeVoe.
- ☐ c. practical joking.
- ☐ d. the summer of 1824.

_____

Supporting Details **3** Lozier and DeVoe planned to save Manhattan's
- ☐ a. southern end.
- ☐ b. eastern end.
- ☐ c. northern end.
- ☐ d. western end.

_____

Conclusion **4** It is evident that Lozier and DeVoe
- ☐ a. were scientists.
- ☐ b. were not taken seriously.
- ☐ c. had unusual senses of humor.
- ☐ d. were construction engineers.

_____

Clarifying Devices **5** The writer treats the subject of the passage with
- ☐ a. deadly seriousness.
- ☐ b. obvious admiration.
- ☐ c. good humor.
- ☐ d. disapproval.

_____

Vocabulary in Context **6** Outrageous in this passage means
- ☐ a. cruel.
- ☐ b. filled with anger.
- ☐ c. fantastic.
- ☐ d. humorless.

_____

Add your scores for questions 1–6. Enter the total here and on the graph on page 237.

Total Score ☐

42

A Blaze of Glory

At night you may see a fireball streak across the sky, or a star may appear to burst and fall. These are both examples of meteors—bits of dust or rock from space that burn up and present fiery <u>spectacles</u> as they strike the earth's atmosphere. Occasionally a meteor is so big that part of it survives the journey through our atmosphere and falls to earth. It is then called a meteorite.

In August of 1971, a meteorite crashed through the roof of a storehouse on a farm in Finland. Farmer Tor-Erik Andersson heard a loud noise, and, rushing to the storehouse, found a dark grey rock about the size of a plum. Through its thin, cracked crust, Tor could see a concretelike inner core. Tor picked the object up and found it to be unusually heavy for its size.

A few months earlier, a similar meteorite had crashed through the roof of Paul Cassarino's home in Wethersfield, Connecticut. This meteorite was a small black rock. It, too, was unusually heavy for its size. Sky watchers had spotted this meteorite when it was still in the meteor stage. About an hour before it landed in Wethersfield, it was observed as a streak of light shooting through the sky above Connecticut.

Meteors are beautiful and exciting sights, and when they crash to earth as meteorites they are both frightening and fascinating. Scientists find meteorites very interesting, too, because meteorites provide them with an opportunity to study materials from outer space without the expense of space travel.

Main Idea 1

	Answer	Score
Mark the *main idea* →	M	15
Mark the statement that is *too broad* →	B	5
Mark the statement that is *too narrow* →	N	5

a. Meteorites are valuable for scientific study. ☐ ____

b. Meteors and meteorites are bits of dust and rocks from space, which travel into the earth's atmosphere. ☐ ____

c. Matter from outer space often travels through the earth's atmosphere. ☐ ____

Subject Matter **2** In general, this passage is about

☐ a. space travel.
☐ b. meteors and meteorites.
☐ c. watching the sky at night.
☐ d. small rocks. _____

Supporting Details **3** One interesting thing about meteorites is

☐ a. they always crash through roofs.
☐ b. we cannot see them at night.
☐ c. they are made of iron.
☐ d. they are often heavy for their size. _____

Conclusion **4** From the passage, we can assume that

☐ a. meteorites never land in South America.
☐ b. not all meteors make it through the earth's atmosphere.
☐ c. buildings are flimsy in Finland.
☐ d. scientists do not like space travel. _____

Clarifying Devices **5** The writer develops the story by using

☐ a. descriptions of real incidents.
☐ b. an analogy.
☐ c. many statistics.
☐ d. negative arguments. _____

Vocabulary in Context **6** In this passage, the word <u>spectacles</u> means

☐ a. eyeglasses.
☐ b. stage shows.
☐ c. displays.
☐ d. stars. _____

Add your scores for questions 1-6. Enter the total here and on the graph on page 237. **Total Score** ☐

43

An Aerodynamic Failure

Aerodynamics is a science that seeks to answer questions about the motion of air relative to solid objects that are in motion. Building a safe airplane, for example, requires an in-depth knowledge of aerodynamics.

Bridge designers must also know about aerodynamics if they are to make safe bridges. Unfortunately, the engineers who designed the Tacoma Narrows Bridge in the state of Washington didn't know quite as much about aerodynamics as they thought they did.

The opening of the bridge in 1940 was celebrated as a great achievement. At the time, the 2,800-foot suspension bridge was the third longest in the world. The celebration, however, was short-lived, for the bridge had serious aerodynamic faults.

The wind proved to be the construction engineers' <u>nemesis</u>. High winds swayed and buckled the new bridge and bewildered the engineers. What had been hailed as a great achievement slowly became a public safety hazard, not to mention a public embarrassment. Finally, several months after the ill-fated bridge went up, it blew apart in forty-five-mile-an-hour winds. No one was injured, but the disaster sent the engineers back to the drawing board.

The second Tacoma Narrows Bridge was aerodynamically sound when it was completed in 1952. Today it stands as the world's longest bridge.

		Answer	Score
Main Idea 1			
Mark the *main idea*	→	M	15
Mark the statement that is *too broad*	→	B	5
Mark the statement that is *too narrow*	→	N	5

a. The Tacoma Narrows Bridge collapsed because it was not aerodynamically sound. ☐ _____

b. Bridges cannot hold up if they are not aerodynamically sound. ☐ _____

c. The Tacoma Narrows Bridge blew apart when it was only a few months old. ☐ _____

Score 15 points for each correct answer. **Score**

Subject Matter
2 This passage is about the
☐ a. day of the Tacoma Narrows Bridge disaster.
☐ b. science of aerodynamics.
☐ c. longest bridge in the world.
☐ d. fateful history of the Tacoma Narrows Bridge.
_____

Supporting Details
3 The second Tacoma Narrows Bridge is
☐ a. the longest in the world.
☐ b. the largest in the U.S.
☐ c. the third longest in the world.
☐ d. longer than the George Washington Bridge.
_____

Conclusion
4 It is evident from the passage that
☐ a. the engineers were totally incompetent.
☐ b. bridges are easy to build.
☐ c. there was still much that wasn't known about aerodynamics in 1940.
☐ d. Washington is a windy state.
_____

Clarifying Devices
5 In the third paragraph, *however* is used to indicate an idea that is
☐ a. similar to those before it.
☐ b. different from those before it.
☐ c. mixed.
☐ d. funny.
_____

Vocabulary in Context
6 A <u>nemesis</u> is a(n)
☐ a. ally.
☐ b. enemy.
☐ c. job.
☐ d. problem.
_____

Add your scores for questions 1-6. Enter the total here and on the graph on page 237.

Total Score ☐

44

Another Look at Spiders

Most people hate spiders. But few consider that spiders are intelligent, inventive and good friends to people.

Spiders have highly developed nervous systems. Their brains are capable of remembering, and they are remarkable engineers. They can be found living anywhere from 22,000 feet above sea level, on Mount Everest, to 2,000 feet below the earth's surface, in caves.

The silk that spiders spin for their webs has a stretching strength superior to most flexible products made by people. These webs have been known to entangle and hold animals as large as mice. The bola spider, instead of making a web, constructs a silken trapeze, which it hangs from branches or twigs. It attaches a globule of sticky silk to the end of the trapeze and casts it out at passing insects. Any insect that gets stuck to the swinging ball becomes the spider's next meal.

One Eurasian species of spider actually travels underwater by carrying a tiny bubble of air with it. Its home is a cozy diving bell constructed from a tightly woven sheet of silk, filled with air bubbles.

Many scientists feel that without the spider human life would be in danger. You see, most of a spider's energies are <u>devoted</u> to catching and eating insects. Without spiders, insects would multiply and cover the earth, destroying the vegetation. It has been estimated that each year spiders in England destroy an amount of insects equal in weight to the human population of that country!

Main Idea	1		Answer	Score
		Mark the *main idea* ⟶	M	15
		Mark the statement that is *too broad* ⟶	B	5
		Mark the statement that is *too narrow* ⟶	N	5
		a. Spiders are highly inventive and extremely helpful to people.	☐	_____
		b. Spiders live and feed in many unusual places.	☐	_____
		c. Some creatures are helpful to people.	☐	_____

Score 15 points for each correct answer.   Score

Subject
Matter

2 The <u>best</u> alternate title for this passage would be

☐ a. What Spiders Eat.

☐ b. The Spider with a Trapeze.

☐ c. The Spider—Nature's Great Engineer.

☐ d. The Spider's Web.   _____

Supporting
Details

3 The bola spider

☐ a. lives underwater.

☐ b. lives in caves.

☐ c. constucts a trapeze.

☐ d. catches mice in its web.   _____

Conclusion

4 We can conclude from the passage that

☐ a. there will soon be more spiders than insects.

☐ b. people should appreciate spiders more.

☐ c. spiders are smarter than human beings.

☐ d. all spiders can live underwater.   _____

Clarifying
Devices

5 The word *but* in the second sentence introduces

☐ a. a clarification.

☐ b. an argument.

☐ c. an exception.

☐ d. a contradiction.   _____

Vocabulary
in Context

6 In this passage <u>devoted</u> means

☐ a. loving.

☐ b. given to.

☐ c. adoring.

☐ d. loyal.   _____

Add your scores for questions 1-6. Enter the total here and on the graph on page 237.   Total
Score ☐

45

What an Actor!

There isn't much likelihood of an uneducated, untrained man being hired to do three very different, highly professional jobs in his life. But a man named Ferdinand Waldo Demera accomplished just that. He was such a <u>consummate</u> actor that he wrote his own roles and played them out upon life's broad stage.

Demera realized early that the only way he could succeed in life would be by using his special powers of deceit. To convince people of his qualifications, Demera forged signatures on an impressive array of references. Then his confident manner and convincing acting made him a success at almost everything he tried. As a surgeon on a Royal Canadian ship during the Korean War, Demera performed nineteen successful operations—and he had had no medical training.

Later, acting as a college professor in applied psychology, he was well liked and admired by both students and faculty. But the day came when Demera's charade was uncovered, so, he kept a low profile for several years. Then he obtained a position as a guidance counselor in a prison. True to form, Demera turned in a very good performance and actually helped many of the inmates.

Demera's trickery eventually became well known, and the story of this highly successful "acting" career was written. Hollywood bought the story and made it into a movie. It was rumored that Demera applied for the lead in his own life's story, but, ironically, he did not pass the screen test. It was the first time he failed to fool.

Main Idea	1		Answer	Score
		Mark the *main idea* →	**M**	15
		Mark the statement that is *too broad* →	**B**	5
		Mark the statement that is *too narrow* →	**N**	5
		a. Demera's life story was made into a movie.	☐	____
		b. Some people are very good actors and can fake their way through life.	☐	____
		c. Demera fooled people into believing he was a trained professional, and successfully held some high-level jobs.	☐	____

Subject Matter **2** This passage describes

☐ a. a life of crime.

☐ b. the life of Ferdinand Demera.

☐ c. a professional Hollywood actor.

☐ d. the talents required for acting.   _____

Supporting Details **3** As a surgeon in the Navy, Demera

☐ a. performed admirably.

☐ b. disgraced himself.

☐ c. performed no operations.

☐ d. was caught and discharged.   _____

Conclusion **4** This passage suggests that Demera might have been an excellent

☐ a. writer.

☐ b. military leader.

☐ c. card player.

☐ d. actor.   _____

Clarifying Devices **5** A person who keeps a "low profile"

☐ a. refuses to speak.

☐ b. wears unattractive clothing.

☐ c. hides from the law.

☐ d. avoids drawing public attention.   _____

Vocabulary in Context **6** Consummate is synonymous with

☐ a. reasonable.

☐ b. skilled.

☐ c. experienced.

☐ d. old.   _____

Add your scores for questions 1-6. Enter the total here and on the graph on page 237.

Total Score ☐

46

A Well-Balanced Act

Jean Francis Grandet was perhaps the most daring man who ever lived, and perhaps the craziest. His greatest desire was to entertain and amaze people. He measured his success by the number of people who fainted dead away after witnessing his death-defying feats.

Grandet, a blond Frenchman, toured North America in 1859, billing himself as "Blondin." Blondin's gift was superb balance. This talent, coupled with an unquenchable desire to astound his audiences, made Blondin an irresistible performer.

His most famous feat was walking across Niagara Falls on a tight-rope. Blondin's "stage" consisted of a three-inch rope strung 1,100 feet across the falls. The rope hung some 160 feet above the jagged rocks and boiling water below the falls.

Simply walking across the falls was not exciting enough for Blondin; he later had to ride across on a bicycle. Then, in another performance, he calmly walked across blindfolded. At still another time, he carried his terrified manager on his back and strolled over the falls before thousands of breathless spectators.

But Blondin was undoubtedly his own worst critic. He was never satisfied with his act and always strove to over-thrill his audience with his balancing wizardry. One of his most daring walks was made in the darkness of night. Blondin became so famous on his tour through North America that his last performance was attended by an admiring Prince of Wales.

Main Idea	1		Answer	Score
		Mark the *main idea* ⟶	M	15
		Mark the statement that is *too broad* ⟶	B	5
		Mark the statement that is *too narrow* ⟶	N	5
		a. Blondin performed death-defying feats that thrilled and amazed audiences.	☐	____
		b. Tightrope performers once amazed audiences by performing fearful balancing acts.	☐	____
		c. Blondin walked across Niagara Falls on a tightrope.	☐	____

Subject Matter

2 This passage is about

- ☐ a. circus performers.
- ☐ b. a balancing daredevil.
- ☐ c. a trapeze artist.
- ☐ d. a foolish Frenchman. _____

Supporting Details

3 Jean Francis Grandet probably performed as "Blondin" because

- ☐ a. he was a show-off.
- ☐ b. he was from France.
- ☐ c. he was blond.
- ☐ d. his manager had suggested the name. _____

Conclusion

4 The passage suggests that Blondin

- ☐ a. was not very intelligent.
- ☐ b. did not like Americans.
- ☐ c. performed as a teenager.
- ☐ d. loved his audiences. _____

Clarifying Devices

5 The writer stimulates the reader's interest by

- ☐ a. using exotic language.
- ☐ b. using a surprise ending.
- ☐ c. describing Blondin's amazing feats.
- ☐ d. asking questions. _____

Vocabulary in Context

6 As used in this passage, <u>billing</u> means to

- ☐ a. charge a price.
- ☐ b. imagine oneself as something.
- ☐ c. spread rumors.
- ☐ d. advertise oneself. _____

Add your scores for questions 1-6. Enter the total here and on the graph on page 237. **Total Score** ☐

47

Barracuda, Eels and Fish

Anyone who enjoys watching colorful fish in an aquarium would really get a thrill out of swimming around a coral reef. Coral reefs are the natural homes of many of the brightly colored tropical fish sold in pet stores. They are formed in warm, shallow seas and provide homes for countless small sea plants, mollusks and crustaceans, which, in turn, feed a host of fishes.

A swimmer or diver among the coral will easily spot the striking black and yellow pattern of the black angelfish, and the many bright colors—yellow, red, green and blue—of parrot fish. Smaller fish such as blueheads, yellow grunts and butterfly fish swarm around the fantastic shapes of the coral—and the predators that feed on them swim here too. The viciously toothed head of a moray eel can be seen peering from a crack. A thin, torpedo-like shape that coasts slowly above the reef is that solitary hunter, the barracuda. Entire schools of the predatory grey snapper patrol the borders of the reef, looking for fish, crabs or shrimp to add to their diet. The colorful and graceful fish of the coral reef include a wide range of types, from the delicate beauty of the little seaweed grazers to the deadly, streamlined shapes of the killers.

Main Idea 1

	Answer	Score
Mark the *main idea* ⟶	M	15
Mark the statement that is *too broad* ⟶	B	5
Mark the statement that is *too narrow* ⟶	N	5

a. Coral reefs are the hunting grounds of moray eels and barracudas. ☐ _____

b. The oceans are filled with an enormous variety of sea plants and animals. ☐ _____

c. Coral reefs are the homes of many kinds of tropical fish. ☐ _____

Score 15 points for each correct answer. **Score**

Subject
Matter **2** This passage deals with
- ☐ a. swimmers and scuba divers.
- ☐ b. coral reefs.
- ☐ c. fishes of the coral reefs.
- ☐ d. schools of fish.

_____

Supporting
Details **3** Coral cannot be found in
- ☐ a. tropical waters.
- ☐ b. the Caribbean.
- ☐ c. the Arctic Ocean.
- ☐ d. shallow waters.

_____

Conclusion **4** The author admires
- ☐ a. the variety of colors in a coral reef.
- ☐ b. warm, shallow seas.
- ☐ c. the daring diver who seeks adventure.
- ☐ d. the size of the coral reefs.

_____

Clarifying
Devices **5** The writer describes the beauty of life among the coral reefs by using
- ☐ a. comparisons.
- ☐ b. supporting statements.
- ☐ c. adjectives.
- ☐ d. contrasts.

_____

Vocabulary
in Context **6** A <u>predatory</u> fish is one that
- ☐ a. is foolish.
- ☐ b. eats other creatures.
- ☐ c. swims fast.
- ☐ d. is protective.

_____

Add your scores for questions 1-6. Enter the total here and on the graph on page 237. **Total Score** ☐

48

The Story of the Hamburger

It would be hard to find a person in America who has never eaten a hamburger, but this popular food was not originally made in America. The original hamburger can be traced back to the Middle Ages, when Russians ate raw meat that was scraped and shredded with a dull knife and formed into patties. It was called Tartar steak. This was the first step in a long series of developments that eventually resulted in hamburger as we know it today.

German sailors picked up the raw meat delicacy in their contacts with Russians and brought it back to their home port of Hamburg. But the people there were not accustomed to eating raw meat, so they broiled the outside of the Russian steak; and so the hamburg steak was born.

The hamburg steak was brought to America in the nineteenth century, by German immigrants. Louis Lassen, a cook in New Haven, Connecticut, modified the hamburg steak by sandwiching it between two pieces of bread. But the true American hamburger came into existence in St. Louis, at the Louisiana Purchase Exposition in 1904. A harried cook at the fair quickly slapped broiled beef patties between buns and served them to a demanding crowd, which gulped them down joyously.

At first this new food creation was made from scraps of poorer cuts of meat that were not used for anything else, but before long scraps were not enough. The demand for greater quantities of hamburger could only be met by using the whole cow. Hamburger stands sprang up all over the country, and a side industry of condiments, such as ketchup and relish, grew up and prospered along with the popular hamburger.

Main Idea	1		Answer	Score
	Mark the *main idea* ⟶		M	15
	Mark the statement that is *too broad* ⟶		B	5
	Mark the statement that is *too narrow* ⟶		N	5
	a. The hamburger is a popular food.		☐	___
	b. The history of the hamburger is a very long one.		☐	___
	c. German sailors brought shredded meat home to Hamburg from Russia.		☐	___

Subject Matter

2 Another good title for this passage would be

☐ a. The St. Louis Fair.
☐ b. Russian Eating Habits.
☐ c. The Development of the Hamburger.
☐ d. The First Hamburger Stand.   _____

Supporting Details

3 The hamburg steak was first introduced in America by

☐ a. Russian soldiers.
☐ b. German immigrants.
☐ c. a St. Louis cook.
☐ d. foreign sailors.   _____

Conclusion

4 We can assume that the citizens of Hamburg

☐ a. liked only fresh raw meat.
☐ b. thought the Russians very clever.
☐ c. were slow in taking on new customs.
☐ d. found raw meat unappetizing.   _____

Clarifying Devices

5 The writer talks about the emergence of the hamburger by

☐ a. retelling Russian folk tales.
☐ b. describing eyewitness accounts.
☐ c. describing the changes step by step.
☐ d. showing that other foods changed, too.   _____

Vocabulary in Context

6 Harried here means

☐ a. busy.
☐ b. careless.
☐ c. lazy.
☐ d. sloppy.   _____

Add your scores for questions 1-6. Enter the total here and on the graph on page 237.   **Total Score** ☐

49

In Memory of William Congreve

With his use of comic dialogue and his satire on upper class society, the playwright William Congreve was the major shaping force of the English comedy of manners. It appears that Congreve was an influential figure in his private life as well, judging by the behavior of his mistress, Henrietta, the second Duchess of Marlborough.

Henrietta and Congreve were devoted companions in the playwright's later years, and when he died he left the Duchess most of his large fortune. But wealth was a cold comfort to the lonely woman, and she became somewhat deranged at the loss of her lover. She had a mask made of Congreve's face and attached it to a life-size dummy. For the rest of her life, the mannequin was her constant companion.

Henrietta required her visitors to bow and greet the dummy and to converse with it as if it were Congreve. The Duchess dressed the mannequin each day, and undressed it each night. She held conversations with the effigy regularly, and her servants waited on it as they would the lord of the manner. Poor Henrietta even called in doctors when she believed the image to be ill. The Duchess's will ordered that upon her death the mannequin be buried with her in her coffin.

Except for the obviously sad and pathetic aspect of the disturbed woman's behavior, Congreve might have viewed the situation as perfect material for one of his own comedies.

Main Idea	1		Answer	Score
	Mark the *main idea*	→	M	15
	Mark the statement that is *too broad*	→	B	5
	Mark the statement that is *too narrow*	→	N	5

a. Mentally unbalanced by Congreve's death, the Duchess of Marlborough had a mannequin made to take his place. ☐ ____

b. The death of a loved one can have a powerful influence on behavior. ☐ ____

c. William Congreve was an important influence on Henrietta, the Duchess of Marlborough. ☐ ____

Subject Matter

2 The passage is primarily about the

☐ a. English comedy of manners.
☐ b. playwright William Congreve.
☐ c. Duchess of Marlborough's reaction to Congreve's death.
☐ d. relationship between Henrietta and Congreve.

_____

Supporting Details

3 The Duchess of Marlborough did <u>not</u>

☐ a. will her fortune to the mannequin.
☐ b. dress and undress the mannequin.
☐ c. have doctors examine the mannequin.
☐ d. hold conversations with the Congreve mannequin.

_____

Conclusion

4 The writer's attitude toward Henrietta's behavior might best be described as one of

☐ a. sarcasm.
☐ b. disapproval.
☐ c. revulsion.
☐ d. pity.

_____

Clarifying Devices

5 The use of the phrase "obviously sad and pathetic" to describe Henrietta's behavior reveals

☐ a. Congreve's attitude toward the Duchess.
☐ b. the writer's feelings about Henrietta.
☐ c. that Henrietta knew that the mannequin was not really Congreve.
☐ d. that the Duchess was undeniably insane.

_____

Vocabulary in Context

6 The best substitution for the word <u>effigy</u> is

☐ a. companion.
☐ b. visitor.
☐ c. figure.
☐ d. object.

_____

Add your scores for questions 1-6. Enter the total here and on the graph on page 237.

Total Score ☐

50

The Fiery Fields

The volcanic eruption of Mount Vesuvius in A.D. 79 covered the entire city of Pompeii with lava and ash. In this great tragedy, people were buried by the thousands, unexpectedly, as they went about their daily work. When the lost city was discovered centuries later, casts of human figures were found in the hardened lava. They were forms of people who had been frozen in action, like actors in a play who suddenly stopped moving.

In the spring of 1970, the people of Pozzuoli, Italy, feared a similar catastrophe. The city lies on top of a volcano that has been slowly pushing its way upward. One area at the edge of the city is known as the "fiery fields." Steam from the hot lava deep down in the earth rises up through cracks in the sidewalks and from the soil.

The "Pozzuoli Uplift" of 1970 was actually a slow earthquake. A large mass of underground lava pushed the soil up three feet in some places. Imagine strolling along a sidewalk and having it rise up in front of you!

Although the damage done was not <u>extensive</u>, people began to panic. Hundreds fled the city, seeking a place of safety. Living in Pozzuoli when the volcano is boiling and the lava is flowing underground is something like living on a ship. When one feels the gentle rocking caused by the waves of lava and steam deep below the earth's surface, one immediately hopes and prays that the waves are not a prelude to a devastating storm.

Main Idea   1

	Answer	Score
Mark the *main idea* ⟶	M	15
Mark the statement that is *too broad* ⟶	B	5
Mark the statement that is *too narrow* ⟶	N	5

a. The people of Pozzuoli are living atop a live volcano. ☐ _____

b. The Pozzuoli Uplift made people fearful of a volcanic eruption. ☐ _____

c. All volcanoes, alive or dormant, are dangerous. ☐ _____

Score 15 points for each correct answer.   **Score**

Subject Matter

2 This passage is mostly about

☐ a. steaming sidewalks.
☐ b. Mount Vesuvius.
☐ c. the volcanic danger in Pozzuoli.
☐ d. Pompeii.

_____

Supporting Details

3 The "fiery fields" are part of

☐ a. a science fiction movie.
☐ b. the area that surrounds Pozzuoli.
☐ c. the damage done by Mount Vesuvius.
☐ d. the city of Pompeii.

_____

Conclusion

4 Although the damage in 1970 was not extensive, it

☐ a. caused great panic.
☐ b. destroyed important documents.
☐ c. was ignored by people who were unafraid.
☐ d. came before a great catastrophe.

_____

Clarifying Devices

5 The content of this passage can best be described as

☐ a. opinionated.
☐ b. informative.
☐ c. argumentative.
☐ d. critical.

_____

Vocabulary in Context

6 As used in this passage, extensive most nearly means

☐ a. far-reaching.
☐ b. unusual.
☐ c. geological.
☐ d. volcanic.

_____

Add your scores for questions 1-6. Enter the total here and on the graph on page 237.

Total Score ☐

51

A Great Tragedy

Margaret Mitchell, the author of the enormously popular novel *Gone With the Wind*, died in 1949, at the age of forty-nine. She was killed by a reckless driver whose only excuse for his carelessness was "everybody does it."

"Peggy" Mitchell wrote her only book in 1936. It won a Pulitzer Prize, and the motion picture adaptation won the Academy Award for best picture, in 1939.

In the summer of 1949, Margaret Mitchell had been considering beginning to write again. Before she could begin another work, however, she was killed while crossing a street in her hometown of Atlanta, Georgia. She and her husband were on their way to see the film *A Canterbury Tale*. As they were crossing the avenue to the theater, a car driven by twenty-nine-year-old, off-duty taxi driver named Hugh D. Gravitt tore around the corner. It braked, skidded and swerved as the driver attempted to avoid the <u>imminent</u> disaster. But Miss Mitchell panicked, pulled away from her husband, and ran in the direction the car had veered. She was hit and fell unconscious. She died of a skull fracture after five days in critical condition.

The driver was sentenced to eighteen months in prison for involuntary manslaughter. He had already been arrested twenty-eight times in the previous ten years for reckless driving. Eight of the arrests had resulted in convictions. Yet, on the day after his conviction for the manslaughter of Margaret Mitchell, and the day before he was to begin serving his sentence, he and his wife were injured when he crashed into a truck.

Main Idea	1		Answer	Score
	Mark the *main idea* ⟶		M	15
	Mark the statement that is *too broad* ⟶		B	5
	Mark the statement that is *too narrow* ⟶		N	5
	a. Margaret Mitchell died without realizing her potential.		☐	____
	b. Carelessness in driving can have tragic results.		☐	____
	c. Margaret Mitchell died in an accident caused by a reckless driver.		☐	____

Subject Matter

2 This passage deals with

☐ a. the life and death of Margaret Mitchell.

☐ b. Margaret Mitchell's tragic death.

☐ c. the dangers of careless driving.

☐ d. the sometimes disastrous results of fame. _____

Supporting Details

3 Margaret Mitchell

☐ a. was in the process of writing another book at the time of her death.

☐ b. had been too ill to write since her first book.

☐ c. wrote many popular books.

☐ d. had thoughts of beginning another book. _____

Conclusion

4 Gravitt hit Miss Mitchell because

☐ a. he was driving too fast to control his car.

☐ b. he was drunk and reacted too slowly.

☐ c. he didn't see her in time to stop.

☐ d. the brakes failed on the slippery road. _____

Clarifying Devices

5 The tone of the passage toward the driver is one of

☐ a. remorse.

☐ b. anger.

☐ c. disdain.

☐ d. lament. _____

Vocabulary in Context

6 <u>Imminent</u> means

☐ a. infamous.

☐ b. terrible.

☐ c. possible.

☐ d. approaching. _____

Add your scores for questions 1-6. Enter the total here and on the graph on page 237.

Total Score ☐

52

A Fishy Story

Stepping into a puddle of water is common enough, but who could ever imagine stepping into a puddle of fish? In February of 1974, Bill Tapp, an Australian rancher, witnessed a rain of fish that covered his property. How surprised he must have been when he heard the patter of fins on his roof!

What caused this strange occurrence? This is a question that had long puzzled ichthyologists—people who study fish. The answer turned out to be a combination of tornado and thunderstorm.

When it is winter in the Northern Hemisphere, it is fall in Australia. Throughout the autumn season, raging storms arise and rains flood the land. Whirlwinds sweep over Australia like giant vacuum cleaners, collecting seaweed, driftwood and even schools of fish. Strong gales may carry these bits of nature for miles before dropping them on barns, live-stock and astonished people.

Although they seem unusual, fish-falls occur quite frequently in Australia's Northern Territory. When Rancher Bill Tapp was asked to describe the deluge, he casually remarked "They look like perch." His statement is not surprising. The wonders of the natural world are as common as rain. Nature, with its <u>infinite</u> mysteries, can create waterfalls that flow upward, and fish that fall out of the sky.

Main Idea	1		Answer	Score
		Mark the *main idea* →	M	15
		Mark the statement that is *too broad* →	B	5
		Mark the statement that is *too narrow* →	N	5

a. Natural weather conditions often cause strange occurrences. ☐ _____

b. A combination of tornadoes and thunderstorms in Australia sometimes produces a rain of fish. ☐ _____

c. Fish-falls occur during the Australian autumn season. ☐ _____

Score 15 points for each correct answer. **Score**

Subject Matter   **2** What is the subject of this passage?

☐ a. The difficulties encountered by ranchers
☐ b. A rain of fish
☐ c. Australia's Northern Territory
☐ d. The damage done by floods   _____

Supporting Details   **3** Fish-falls occur in Australia

☐ a. on large ranches.
☐ b. only in the winter.
☐ c. quite often.
☐ d. when the air is calm.   _____

Conclusion   **4** What conclusion can you draw from this passage?

☐ a. The seasons in the Southern Hemisphere are reversed.
☐ b. One should watch where one steps.
☐ c. The natural world is full of surprises.
☐ d. Ichthyologists are tireless workers.   _____

Clarifying Devices   **5** Which of the following phrases offers a comparison that helps you visualize something in the passage?

☐ a. A combination of tornado and thunderstorm
☐ b. Whirlwinds are like vacuum cleaners
☐ c. As common as rain
☐ d. The patter of fins on his roof   _____

Vocabulary in Context   **6** The word <u>infinite</u> is closest in meaning to

☐ a. complex.
☐ b. varied.
☐ c. countless.
☐ d. dangerous.   _____

Add your scores for questions 1-6. Enter the total here and on the graph on page 237.   Total Score ☐

127

53

The Amazing Recovery

Some organisms, such as salamanders and lobsters, can regenerate limbs they have lost. This means they can regrow a foot, a tail or any other part of the body that has been cut or broken off. Although human cells are incapable of this, the human body is wonderfully resilient in other ways. For one thing, it can withstand strong blows and still maintain its ability to function. The amazing recovery of Phineas Gage is a case in point.

Phineas P. Gage, who was employed by the Rutland and Burlington Railroad, recovered from an injury that defied medical history. While he was doing repairs on the railroad, a stack of high-powered dynamite accidently exploded. The terrific blast drove a three-foot-long, thirteen-pound iron bar into his head, destroying most of his brain.

Gage was thrown by the explosion, but regained consciousness soon afterward. He even watched the doctors as they tended his wound. For several weeks Gage was disoriented and could not see through his left eye. But in a few months he was able to think clearly and return to work.

Until this day, doctors have found no plausible explanation for this man's recovery. They never expected Gage to survive, but he lived for several years after the accident. After Gage died, his skull was placed in the museum of the Massachusetts Medical College, where it remains as a monument to the human will to live.

Main Idea	1		Answer	Score
	Mark the *main idea*	→	M	15
	Mark the statement that is *too broad*	→	B	5
	Mark the statement that is *too narrow*	→	N	5

a. All living creatures have extremely strong survival mechanisms. ☐ _____

b. Gage withstood a tremendous blow to the head. ☐ _____

c. The human body can be tremendously resilient. ☐ _____

Score 15 points for each correct answer.   **Score**

Subject Matter

2 This passage is primarily about
- [ ] a. regeneration.
- [ ] b. Phineas P. Gage.
- [ ] c. salamanders.
- [ ] d. modern medicine.   _____

Supporting Details

3 Which detail best supports the idea that human beings are very resilient?
- [ ] a. A few months after the accident, Gage returned to work.
- [ ] b. Gage's skull is in a museum.
- [ ] c. Gage was a hard worker.
- [ ] d. Gage could not see through his left eye.   _____

Conclusion

4 We can infer from the passage that
- [ ] a. it takes time to recover from an accident.
- [ ] b. railroad workers must be careful.
- [ ] c. the human will to live is powerful.
- [ ] d. salamanders make good pets.   _____

Clarifying Devices

5 The author develops the main idea by using
- [ ] a. one specific case.
- [ ] b. arguments and proof.
- [ ] c. comparison.
- [ ] d. contrast.   _____

Vocabulary in Context

6 Plausible means
- [ ] a. fearful.
- [ ] b. magical.
- [ ] c. reasonable.
- [ ] d. medical.   _____

Add your scores for questions 1–6. Enter the total here and on the graph on page 237.

Total Score [ ]

54

Billions Waiting to be Found

Almost everyone has heard stories about lucky adventurers finding buried treasure, but few people take treasure hunting seriously. They figure that most lost treasures have already been found by someone. Fortunately, however, for the many serious treasure seekers, there are still plenty of treasures to be found in the United States.

Experts on the subject believe that over four billion dollars in lost treasure is just waiting to be found. The treasure is not all in one place, of course. That would be too easy. A serious treasure hunter must be determined and investigate one particular lost treasure, gathering as many clues about its whereabouts as possible.

Gold, jewels and currency make up most lost treasures. The stories behind these hidden riches are extremely varied and always interesting. For example, during the Civil War, a band of Confederate soldiers robbed a Union bank of $114,000 in gold, which has never been recovered. The infamous outlaw Jesse James stole one million dollars in gold bars which the government never found. Oklahoma would be the place to go looking for that treasure. The notorious pirate Captain Kidd buried $50,000 in gold and jewels on Long Island, New York, in 1699. He was hanged before he could dig it up or tell someone where it was.

Hundreds of other treasures remain to be found. All it takes is a little research, a good map and a lot of good luck.

Main Idea	1		Answer	Score
	Mark the *main idea* ⟶		M	15
	Mark the statement that is *too broad* ⟶		B	5
	Mark the statement that is *too narrow* ⟶		N	5
	a. Most lost treasures consist of gold, jewels and currency.		☐	___
	b. There are still valuable lost treasures to be found in the United States.		☐	___
	c. Many people dream of finding lost treasures.		☐	___

Subject Matter   **2** This passage deals mainly with
- ☐ a. gold mining.
- ☐ b. bank robberies.
- ☐ c. Jesse James.
- ☐ d. lost treasure.   _____

Supporting Details   **3** The value of the treasure still lost in the U.S. is about
- ☐ a. $400,000.
- ☐ b. $4,000,000.
- ☐ c. $18 billion.
- ☐ d. $4 billion.   _____

Conclusion   **4** Judging from this passage, one might say that treasure hunting is
- ☐ a. easy.
- ☐ b. difficult.
- ☐ c. dangerous.
- ☐ d. ridiculous.   _____

Clarifying Devices   **5** The writer builds interest in treasure hunting by
- ☐ a. giving examples of treasures that are still lost.
- ☐ b. describing how to find buried treasure.
- ☐ c. telling humorous stories about treasure hunters.
- ☐ d. citing examples of successful treasure hunters.   _____

Vocabulary in Context   **6** A <u>notorious</u> person
- ☐ a. is well respected.
- ☐ b. has a bad reputation.
- ☐ c. is courageous.
- ☐ d. is cruel.   _____

Add your scores for questions 1–6. Enter the total here and on the graph on page 237.   **Total Score** [ ]

55

Food for Thought

For years fish has been popularly referred to as "brain food" because of the false notion that eating it improved a person's intelligence. Scientists, however, have recently discovered that a more effective form of brain food may be brains themselves!

Experiments were conducted at the University of Michigan to discover if memory could be extracted from one animal and transferred to another. Planarian worms were trained to respond in a certain manner when exposed to light. After their training, the worms were diced and fed to untrained planarian worms, which were then given the same training as their predecessors. The second batch of worms responded to training many times faster than the originals, indicating that knowledge had somehow been transferred from one to the other through the body tissue.

Later, at Baylor University in Alabama, similar experiments were conducted using mice. Mice in one group were trained to find their way through a maze. Then they were killed, and an extract was made from their brains. This extract was fed to untrained mice who then learned to thread through the maze twice as quickly as their predecessors had. However, when these same mice were placed in an altogether different maze, they showed no particular aptitude for finding their way through it. Apparently the acquired knowledge of the first group of mice had been transferred to the second group in the form of food made from their brains.

Perhaps someday real "brain food" will be on the menu in school cafeterias!

Main Idea	1		Answer	Score
		Mark the *main idea* →	M	15
		Mark the statement that is *too broad* →	B	5
		Mark the statement that is *too narrow* →	N	5

a. Knowledge has been transferred experimentally from one animal to another through body tissue. ☐ _____

b. Mice and planaria can be trained to act in certain ways. ☐ _____

c. Experiments on animals can have important results. ☐ _____

Subject Matter

2 This passage is primarily about

☐ a. training mice to run a maze.

☐ b. training planaria to respond to light.

☐ c. the discovery of real "brain food."

☐ d. exotic forms of food.

_____

Supporting Details

3 Untrained planaria that had eaten the trained planaria were

☐ a. able to crawl through a maze more successfully.

☐ b. unable to be trained, no matter how much time was spent with them.

☐ c. trained more quickly to perform the same task.

☐ d. trained more easily to perform different tasks.

_____

Conclusion

4 The last sentence implies that

☐ a. fish may soon be served in schools.

☐ b. planaria may soon be served in schools.

☐ c. experiments may someday produce brain food for humans.

☐ d. the notion of "brain food" is without basis.

_____

Clarifying Devices

5 The sentence containing the phrase "they showed no particular aptitude" explains that the second group of mice

☐ a. had forgotten what they had learned from the first group.

☐ b. had learned the specific knowledge that the first group had about one maze.

☐ c. were less intelligent than the first group.

☐ d. couldn't find their way through mazes.

_____

Vocabulary in Context

6 Another word for predecessors is

☐ a. antagonists.

☐ b. ancestors.

☐ c. forerunners.

☐ d. friends.

_____

Add your scores for questions 1-6. Enter the total here and on the graph on page 237.

Total Score ☐

56

Eyeglasses

How long ago were eyeglasses first used? Theodore Roosevelt was the first president to pose for his official portrait in glasses. Benjamin Franklin, of course, wore wire-rimmed eyeglasses. He was also the inventor of bifocals. As long ago as the 1600s, the famous philosopher Spinoza made lenses for glasses. Before him, Galileo used ground glass, in the form of a telescope, to aid the human eye in exploring the hidden details of the universe.

Eyeglasses in fact were invented as long ago as the 1300s. Eyeglasses may seem out of place on a figure painted in the Middle Ages, but at this time glasses were considered the mark of a person of learning, of someone worthy of respect. In the year 1480, the Italian painter Domenico Ghirlandajo made a portrait of St. Jerome, in which he included spectacles hanging from the saint's desk. Such a detail is remarkable, since St. Jerome died over a thousand years before! Although St. Jerome could not possibly have worn glasses, the artist appended them as a symbol of special dignity. The spectacle maker's guild even made St. Jerome its patron saint.

Spectacles today are made not only of glass, but also of plastic. They may be tinted, sun-sensitive, reflective or cut into fanciful shapes. Contact lenses may be worn invisibly, directly on the eyes. All of these vision improvers are a far cry from the crude, heavy eyeglasses of the fourteenth century!

Main Idea   **1**

	Answer	Score
Mark the *main idea* ⟶	M	15
Mark the statement that is *too broad* ⟶	B	5
Mark the statement that is *too narrow* ⟶	N	5

a. Eyeglasses have a long history, extending back to the 1300s. ☐ _____

b. Eyeglasses were invented long ago. ☐ _____

c. Eyeglasses have become very sophisticated. ☐ _____

Score 15 points for each correct answer.   **Score**

Subject Matter

2 Another good title for this passage would be
- ☐ a. Ben Franklin's Invention.
- ☐ b. The History of Eyeglasses.
- ☐ c. How Far Can People See?
- ☐ d. Galileo's Glasses.

_____

Supporting Details

3 This passage mentions that Benjamin Franklin invented
- ☐ a. bifocals.
- ☐ b. the telescope.
- ☐ c. the first eyeglasses.
- ☐ d. the lightning rod.

_____

Conclusion

4 According to information in this passage, St. Jerome died somewhere around
- ☐ a. the 1300s.
- ☐ b. 1480.
- ☐ c. 480.
- ☐ d. 1600.

_____

Clarifying Devices

5 In the first paragraph, historical figures are listed in
- ☐ a. order of importance.
- ☐ b. random sequence.
- ☐ c. alphabetical order.
- ☐ d. reverse historical order.

_____

Vocabulary in Context

6 Appended, as used in this passage, means
- ☐ a. upset.
- ☐ b. added.
- ☐ c. cut out.
- ☐ d. painted.

_____

Add your scores for questions 1-6. Enter the total here and on the graph on page 237.

Total Score ☐

57

Disaster

The disaster which would give Johnstown, Pennsylvania, a place in history began when it started to rain on the evening of May 30, 1889. All through the night and all the next day the rain poured down, swelling creeks and rivers and filling the reservoir behind the South Fork Dam to overflowing.

At three o'clock in the afternoon on May 31, the Reverend Brown noticed the first break in the face of the old earthen dam and cried, "God have mercy on the people below!" The break quickly widened, and the swollen lake of water in the reservoir behind the dam threw itself into the valley below. The collapse of the dam was so sudden that the water surged downhill in a wall thirty to forty feet high, crushing and carrying along trees, boulders, buildings, railroad cars— everything in its path. When the flood hit a stone bridge fifteen miles downstream in Johnstown, the mass of wreckage jammed into a pile about seventy feet high, creating a dam that caused the water racing behind it to rise and spread <u>debris</u> over thirty acres of land.

More than 2,000 people were killed in the Johnstown flood, making it the worst flood disaster in American history—a record no one wants to see surpassed.

Main Idea	1		Answer	Score
	Mark the *main idea*	→	M	15
	Mark the statement that is *too broad*	→	B	5
	Mark the statement that is *too narrow*	→	N	5

a. Johnstown, Pennsylvania, was flooded on May 31, 1889. ☐ _____

b. Johnstown, Pennsylvania, was the site of a famous disaster. ☐ _____

c. The worst flood in American history was caused by a broken dam in Johnstown, Pennsylvania. ☐ _____

Subject Matter   **2** This passage is primarily about

☐ a. a Memorial Day celebration.
☐ b. dam safety measures.
☐ c. unusually heavy rainfalls.
☐ d. a terrible flood.   _____

Supporting Details   **3** The Johnstown flood is famous because of

☐ a. the number of lives that were lost.
☐ b. the size of the dam that broke.
☐ c. the date on which it happened.
☐ d. the speed at which the flood moved.   _____

Conclusion   **4** What is the most likely reason that no flood has since claimed so many lives?

☐ a. People no longer live near dams.
☐ b. There are fewer heavy rainfalls.
☐ c. Dams are being built more carefully.
☐ d. Towns are now built to survive floods.   _____

Clarifying Devices   **5** The writer quotes the Reverend Brown in order to

☐ a. supply all the facts.
☐ b. add emotional impact.
☐ c. reveal his own bias.
☐ d. support his argument.   _____

Vocabulary in Context   **6** Debris is

☐ a. chaos.
☐ b. disease.
☐ c. terror.
☐ d. wreckage.   _____

Add your scores for questions 1-6. Enter the total here and on the graph on page 237.   **Total Score** ☐

58

Nine Young Prisoners

In 1848, nine young men were convicted of treason against the queen of England. The penalty for this crime was death. These men had to be dealt with strongly, because they could not be allowed to set a bad example for others. Although the people sided with the convicted young men, the judge sentenced them to be hanged.

The court case drew a great deal of public interest, and the nine men became famous. Protests against their punishment were held in the British government. Queen Victoria finally decided not to carry out the death sentence, but instead sentenced them to spend the rest of their lives in the penal colonies of Australia.

This change of sentence was fortunate for everyone, because the nine men all went on to become prominent leaders. One had a brilliant career in United States politics, and his son became mayor of New York City. Another, Tom McGee, became a member of the Canadian House of Commons. Two others became brigadier generals in the Union Army during the Civil War. Richard O'Gormon became the governor general of Newfoundland. Tom Meagher became governor of Montana. Morris Legene became attorney general of Australia, and Michael Ireland succeeded him in that office.

The success of all of the nine men eventually came to the attention of Queen Victoria in a curious way. In 1871, she found herself dealing with the ninth man, the newly elected prime minister of Australia. It was Mr. Charles Duffy, a person whom she had saved from hanging. When she heard of the success of the others, she realized that by cheating the hangman she had enriched humanity.

Main Idea	1		Answer	Score
		Mark the *main idea* ⟶	M	15
		Mark the statement that is *too broad* ⟶	B	5
		Mark the statement that is *too narrow* ⟶	N	5
		a. Convicts who are freed can become great leaders.	☐	___
		b. Queen Victoria spared the lives of nine convicted traitors.	☐	___
		c. Nine convicted traitors were spared their lives and became successful leaders.	☐	___

Subject
Matter

2 This passage is mostly concerned with

- ☐ a. nine English convicts.
- ☐ b. Queen Victoria.
- ☐ c. the English court system.
- ☐ d. Australia's colonies. _____

Supporting
Details

3 The nine men were convicted of

- ☐ a. robbery.
- ☐ b. murder.
- ☐ c. disrespect.
- ☐ d. treason. _____

Conclusion

4 From this passage we can conclude that
Queen Victoria

- ☐ a. was a cold, unfriendly person.
- ☐ b. was a good leader for her country.
- ☐ c. never disagreed with anybody.
- ☐ d. was tolerant of human errors. _____

Clarifying
Devices

5 To say that Queen Victoria "cheated the
hangman" means she

- ☐ a. didn't pay the person who would have
  hung the men.
- ☐ b. lied to the hangman.
- ☐ c. robbed the prisoners of their rights.
- ☐ d. cheated death by not hanging the men. _____

Vocabulary
in Context

6 Prominent, as used here, means

- ☐ a. wealthy.
- ☐ b. political.
- ☐ c. conspicuous.
- ☐ d. important. _____

**Add your scores for questions 1–6. Enter the
total here and on the graph on page 237.**   **Total
Score** ☐

59

Life in the Deep

Strange-looking creatures dwell in the deepest parts of the ocean, where no light ever reaches. One of the inhabitants of this dark, high-pressure underwater <u>habitat</u> is the anglerfish. It has several unusual features.

Since it is so dark in the depths of Davy Jones's Locker, it is very difficult for fish to spot possible prey, or to find mates. The female anglerfish solves the hunting problem by means of a long tentacle of flesh, up to four inches long, which extends upward from the top of her body. This tentacle acts as a fishing pole of sorts: its end emits a glowing light, which, in the pitch darkness, serves to attract smaller fish. The female anglerfish then quickly snaps them up.

Nature has apparently solved the problem of finding a mate by developing a relationship in which the male of the species acts as a parasite to the female. The much smaller male anglerfish attaches itself to a female early in its life, by biting into her flesh. His mouth becomes firmly affixed to the female's skin, and soon they are even sharing the same bloodstream! After this stage has been reached, the male receives its nourishment through the connection to the female, and soon its own digestive organs and other major organs deteriorate. Only the reproductive organs remain intact.

Main Idea	1		Answer	Score
	Mark the *main idea* ⟶	M		15
	Mark the statement that is *too broad* ⟶	B		5
	Mark the statement that is *too narrow* ⟶	N		5

a. The anglerfish has special adaptations that help it live in the darkness of the ocean's depths. ☐ ____

b. Strange-looking creatures live in the depths of the sea. ☐ ____

c. The female anglerfish has a special way of attracting fish. ☐ ____

Score 15 points for each correct answer.   **Score**

Subject
Matter

2 This passage deals mainly with

- ☐ a. deep-sea life.
- ☐ b. interesting facts about anglerfish.
- ☐ c. nature's way of solving problems
      of environment.
- ☐ d. the diet of the anglerfish.   _____

Supporting
Details

3 The tentacle attracts smaller fish because

- ☐ a. they think it is something to eat.
- ☐ b. its waving intrigues them.
- ☐ c. its light is unusual and alluring.
- ☐ d. they think it is seaweed to hide in.   _____

Conclusion

4 It can be assumed from the passage that

- ☐ a. the male anglerfish dies before the
      female.
- ☐ b. the mate-finding problem is solved
      because the mates remain attached to
      each other.
- ☐ c. the small prey of the anglerfish cannot
      escape once they are drawn to the light.
- ☐ d. anglerfish are the biggest in the deep sea.   _____

Clarifying
Devices

5 The anglerfish's "hunting problem," referred to
in the second paragraph, is the problem of

- ☐ a. finding a mate.
- ☐ b. finding fish to eat.
- ☐ c. being hunted by larger fish.
- ☐ d. being caught by fishermen.   _____

Vocabulary
in Context

6 The word <u>habitat</u> means

- ☐ a. environment.
- ☐ b. dangerous area.
- ☐ c. dark area.
- ☐ d. ocean bed.   _____

Add your scores for questions 1–6. Enter the   Total ☐
total here and on the graph on page 237.   Score

60

Beards for All Occasions

Dressing fashionably was very important in fourteenth-century Spain. This was especially true for any man who considered himself an aristocrat or a dandy. Before going out, a well-dressed man would put on his finest boots, one of his embroidered capes and his favorite beard, dyed to match the color of his clothing!

Believe it or not, false beards were once as popular as neckties are today. Beards had for years been considered a sign of strength and manhood, and the bigger and thicker they were, the better. Those unfortunates who had little facial hair were forced by custom into wearing false beards made of horsehair. Soon, however, every man in the Spanish fashion world was wearing them too, while many quite substantial real beards were shaved off to make way for the false variety.

By day, the fashionable dandy might wear a yellow or a crimson beard to impress his friends, but in the evening a long black beard was proper for serenading his senorita. Any color or shape of beard could be had.

However, as you can imagine, the growth of this unusual custom created many interesting problems. People with similar beards were mistaken for one another. Creditors could not find debtors, and police often arrested the wrong people, while the real villains escaped wearing their hairy disguises. The price of horsehair skyrocketed. Finally, King Philip IV of Aragon put a stop to all the foolishness by outlawing the wearing of false beards.

Main Idea	1		Answer	Score
	Mark the *main idea*	→	M	15
	Mark the statement that is *too broad*	→	B	5
	Mark the statement that is *too narrow*	→	N	5

a. In fourteenth-century Spain, false beards were very popular. ☐ _____

b. False beards came in many colors and sizes. ☐ _____

c. People have adapted to many unusual, and sometimes humorous, customs. ☐

Subject Matter　　**2** What is the passage mostly concerned with?

☐ a. The size of beards

☐ b. The color of beards

☐ c. Varieties of false beards

☐ d. The custom of wearing false beards　　_____

Supporting Details　**3** According to the passage, false beards were worn by those who considered themselves to be

☐ a. handsome and mature.

☐ b. too young to have real beards.

☐ c. aristocrats or fashionable dandies.

☐ d. royalty.　　_____

Conclusion　　**4** We can assume from the passage that

☐ a. red beards were more fashionable than black ones.

☐ b. everyone in fourteenth-century Spain shaved.

☐ c. false beards were considered foolish by those who had real beards.

☐ d. the popularity of false beards largely died out after the fourteenth century.　　_____

Clarifying Devices　**5** The writer reveals the "foolishness" of the custom in the last paragraph by

☐ a. giving odd or humorous examples.

☐ b. using convincing arguments.

☐ c. giving eyewitness accounts.

☐ d. saying that Philip IV of Aragon put a stop to it.　　_____

Vocabulary in Context　**6** The best definition for the word <u>unfortunates</u> is

☐ a. those who have no facial hair.

☐ b. those who are unlucky.

☐ c. very young people.

☐ d. very poor people.　　_____

Add your scores for questions 1–6. Enter the total here and on the graph on page 237.　　**Total Score** ☐

61

The Historical Barbecue

During warm weather, a favorite American form of entertainment is the barbecue. Families light up the charcoal and cook chicken, hamburgers and hot dogs to eat "alfresco." Did you know that barbecues have been held for over four hundred years?

The Carib Indians in the West Indies and in northern South America had wooden grills on which they broiled, smoked and dried meat and fish. They called these grills *barbacoas.* The idea was introduced into the United States around 1700.

A barbecue, originally, was simply the roasting or broiling of a large animal, such as a hog or an ox, over an open pit. Later, it came to mean an open-air social or political gathering. George Washington often attended barbecues in Virginia.

Perhaps the biggest barbecue on record was held in 1923, when John Calloway Walton gave a barbecue for 100,000 people, to celebrate his election as governor of Oklahoma. A mile-long trench was dug to roast the beef, pork, mutton, buffalo, bear, reindeer, antelope, squirrel, opossum, coon, rabbit, chicken, goose and duck that was on the menu. In addition, a massive amount of bread and coffee was served. The coffee was made in <u>urns</u> that held 10,000 gallons each. All in all, it was quite a feast.

Main Idea 1

	Answer	Score
Mark the *main idea* ⟶	**M**	15
Mark the statement that is *too broad* ⟶	**B**	5
Mark the statement that is *too narrow* ⟶	**N**	5

a. Americans today enjoy barbecues. ☐ ____

b. Americans like to entertain. ☐ ____

c. The barbecue is an American tradition of long standing. ☐ ____

Subject Matter

2 This selection is mainly about

- [ ] a. the many foods eaten at barbecues.
- [ ] b. the history of the barbecue.
- [ ] c. a Carib Indian's diet.
- [ ] d. the biggest barbecue ever.

_____

Supporting Details

3 At original American barbecues, large animals were roasted

- [ ] a. in an oven.
- [ ] b. over a large fire.
- [ ] c. on a spit.
- [ ] d. over an open pit.

_____

Conclusion

4 The passage implies that

- [ ] a. only Americans have barbecues.
- [ ] b. barbecues are held only on holidays.
- [ ] c. no one went hungry at Calloway's barbecue.
- [ ] d. traditions don't last long.

_____

Clarifying Devices

5 The author shows the history of the barbecue through

- [ ] a. inductive reasoning.
- [ ] b. comparison and contrast.
- [ ] c. historical fact.
- [ ] d. lively description.

_____

Vocabulary in Context

6 An <u>urn</u> is a

- [ ] a. utensil for filling cups.
- [ ] b. large container.
- [ ] c. small bowl.
- [ ] d. barrel.

_____

Add your scores for questions 1-6. Enter the total here and on the graph on page 238.

Total Score ☐

62

How Hollywood Went "Hollywood"

The land of tinsel and glitter hasn't always shone as brightly as it does today. For most people, Hollywood means movies, glamour and fast living. Yet, this commonly held image of the city of the stars could not be farther from what the town's founders intended.

Horace Wilcox, the leader of the Temperance Society, was one of the early developers of the area. His wife gave Hollywood its name. After acquiring the land for the community in 1887, Wilcox established an orchard, built homes and churches, and planned for parks and libraries. Intending the village to be a model community, Wilcox and the Society declared that only those who <u>abstained</u> from alcohol could settle there.

Hollywood existed as its founders intended for over twenty years. In 1900, there were fewer than 500 residents. No one carried firearms and there was no jail, as crime was practically nonexistent. The mayor served without pay, as a public service, and the town's trustees met only once a year.

But this quiet and bliss was destined to end. In 1910, the residents voted to join with the city of Los Angeles, in order to gain access to the city's water supply. The following year, the first motion picture studio was established, and from then on the industry grew rapidly.

Hollywood today is universally considered the movie capital of the world. With its population of over 200,000 and its image of opulence and excess, the city is a far cry from the model temperance community of its origins.

		Answer	Score
Main Idea 1			
Mark the *main idea*	→	M	15
Mark the statement that is *too broad*	→	B	5
Mark the statement that is *too narrow*	→	N	5
a. In the early 1900s, Hollywood was a small town.		☐	___
b. Hollywood has become a very different community from what its founders intended.		☐	___
c. Like many towns that were once small, Hollywood has changed.		☐	___

Score 15 points for each correct answer.   Score

Subject Matter

2 The best alternate title for the passage would be
- [ ] a. Horace Wilcox, Founder of Hollywood.
- [ ] b. Hollywood—Then and Now.
- [ ] c. The Temperance Movement.
- [ ] d. Hollywood—Movie Capital of the World.   _____

Supporting Details

3 Hollywood was named by
- [ ] a. Horace Wilcox.
- [ ] b. members of the Temperance Society.
- [ ] c. the early residents of the town.
- [ ] d. Horace Wilcox's wife.   _____

Conclusion

4 According to the passage, what event seems to have opened the way for movie studios in Hollywood?
- [ ] a. The expansion of the movie industry
- [ ] b. Horace Wilcox's death
- [ ] c. The residents' vote to join the city of Los Angeles
- [ ] d. A sudden growth in Hollywood's population   _____

Clarifying Devices

5 As used in the first paragraph, *yet* indicates
- [ ] a. an explanation.
- [ ] b. a contrasting idea.
- [ ] c. a similar event.
- [ ] d. an example.   _____

Vocabulary in Context

6 Abstained means
- [ ] a. didn't sell.
- [ ] b. didn't like the taste of.
- [ ] c. refrained from drinking.
- [ ] d. used wisely.   _____

Add your scores for questions 1-6. Enter the total here and on the graph on page 238.   Total Score [ ]

63

Why Do They Do It?

Why would an animal commit suicide? It seems a strange question, and yet it is one that has intrigued some people for a long time. For there is a kind of rodent, called the lemming, which periodically commits mass suicide, and no one knows just why!

These small creatures, which inhabit the Scandinavian mountains, sustain themselves on a diet of roots and moss, and live in nests they burrow underground. When their food supply is sufficiently large, the lemmings live a normal, undisturbed rodent life.

However, when the lemmings' food supply becomes too low to support the population, a <u>singular</u> migration commences—the lemmings leave their burrows en masse, forming huge hordes. Great numbers of the rodents begin a trek across the Scandinavian plains. The journey may last weeks. The lemmings devour everything in their path, continuing their destructive march until they reach the sea.

The reason for what follows remains an enigma for zoologists and naturalists. Upon reaching the coast, the lemmings do not stop. They swim by the thousands into the surf. They stay afloat for only a short time before they tire, sink and drown. Thousands upon thousands of the little animals die in this rush to the sea.

A common theory for this mass suicide is that the lemmings do not realize that the ocean is such a huge body of water. In their cross-country journey, the animals must traverse many smaller bodies of water, such as rivers and small lakes. They may assume that the sea is just another such swimmable obstacle. But no final answer has been found to the mystery.

Main Idea	1		Answer	Score
		Mark the *main idea* ⟶	M	15
		Mark the statement that is *too broad* ⟶	B	5
		Mark the statement that is *too narrow* ⟶	N	5
		a. It is unusual for animals to commit suicide.	☐	___
		b. Lemmings periodically march to the sea and inexplicably drown themselves in vast numbers.	☐	___
		c. Lemmings go on a long march when their food supply gets too low.	☐	___

Subject Matter

2 This passage is about

☐ a. how lemmings find food.

☐ b. the concept of animal suicide.

☐ c. the phenomenon of the lemming "suicide."

☐ d. the food supply in the Scandinavian mountains.

_____

Supporting Details

3 A reason for the lemmings' self-destruction might be that they

☐ a. go mad from a lack of food.

☐ b. hope to find fish for food.

☐ c. decide to thin out the population.

☐ d. think they can cross the sea.

_____

Conclusion

4 Scientists are intrigued by the lemmings' behavior because

☐ a. they are the only rodents that live in Scandinavia.

☐ b. it is very unusual for animals to commit suicide.

☐ c. of the amount of food they can eat on their march to the sea.

☐ d. they can gather together in such huge numbers.

_____

Clarifying Devices

5 The word *however*, in the first sentence of the third paragraph, signals that the information that follows is

☐ a. merely a detail.

☐ b. in contrast to preceding information.

☐ c. similar to preceding information.

☐ d. an example related to preceding information.

_____

Vocabulary in Context

6 In this passage <u>singular</u> means

☐ a. unusual.

☐ b. solitary.

☐ c. temporary.

☐ d. individual.

_____

Add your scores for questions 1–6. Enter the total here and on the graph on page 238.

Total Score ☐

64

Just a Coincidence?

Since 1840, every American president elected in the twentieth year—Harrison 1840, Lincoln 1860, Garfield 1880, McKinley 1900, Harding 1920, Roosevelt 1940, and Kennedy 1960—has died in office. Is this, as people often say, "just a coincidence"?

There are very strong parallels between the careers of Presidents Lincoln and Kennedy. Lincoln was first elected to Congress in 1846, Kennedy in 1946. Both men had been in the armed forces. Each worked for the cause of civil rights. Both presidents were assassinated. Lincoln was killed by a man born in 1839 and Kennedy by one born in 1939. Both assassins were Southerners who were killed before they could be tried.

The assassinations both occurred on Fridays, with the wives of the presidents present. Lincoln had a secretary named Kennedy who told him not to go to the theatre. President Kennedy's secretary, a Mrs. Lincoln, warned him against visiting Dallas, where he was shot.

Southerners named Johnson (Andrew, born in 1808 and Lyndon, born in 1908) succeeded both Lincoln and Kennedy.

With more digging, no doubt, more of these similarities could be found. Do people find coincidences where they look for them? Perhaps. At any rate, if John Kennedy had been aware of the similar details of Abraham Lincoln's life, he might have listened to his secretary and cancelled his fateful Dallas trip.

Main Idea	1			Answer	Score
		Mark the *main idea* ⟶		M	15
		Mark the statement that is *too broad* ⟶		B	5
		Mark the statement that is *too narrow* ⟶		N	5

a. There are amazing similarities in the details of the lives of many American presidents. ☐ _____

b. The circumstances of Lincoln's and Kennedy's deaths were very similar. ☐ _____

c. There are many striking parallels in the histories of Kennedy and Lincoln. ☐ _____

Score 15 points for each correct answer. **Score**

Subject Matter

2 The best alternate title for this passage would be

☐ a. American Presidents.
☐ b. The Lincoln and Kennedy Assassinations.
☐ c. The Careers of Lincoln and Kennedy.
☐ d. Lincoln and Kennedy: Striking Similarities.

_____

Supporting Details

3 The secretaries of both Lincoln and Kennedy

☐ a. saw the assassinations.
☐ b. were named Johnson.
☐ c. advised them not to go to the places where they were killed.
☐ d. were born in years ending in "39."

_____

Conclusion

4 The writer seems to think that coincidences

☐ a. definitely have hidden meanings.
☐ b. may or may not occur simply by chance.
☐ c. are always found wherever people look for them.
☐ d. do not occur very often.

_____

Clarifying Devices

5 The first paragraph catches the reader's attention with a

☐ a. surprising fact.
☐ b. vivid adjective.
☐ c. first-hand story.
☐ d. broad generalization.

_____

Vocabulary in Context

6 As used in this passage, <u>succeeded</u> is closest in meaning to

☐ a. achieved.
☐ b. came before.
☐ c. broke away from.
☐ d. came after.

_____

Add your scores for questions 1–6. Enter the total here and on the graph on page 238.

Total Score ☐

65

A Natural Contract

It's practically a business arrangement. A symbiosis is a partnership between two living organisms, which benefits both of the organisms. Nature provides us with many extraordinary examples of symbiosis in the animal kingdom.

It's not an unusual sight in Africa to see a tiny bird, the egret, standing <u>confidently</u> atop the massive back of a rhinocerous. This powerful, and sometimes fierce, animal doesn't at all mind giving the little bird a free ride. Egrets help their larger partners by cleaning them of harmful ticks and fleas. In return, they get a free meal. The rhino and the egret constitute a symbiotic partnership.

Another bird, called the plover, lives its life happily walking up and down the length of a crocodile's back. The crocodile doesn't object because the plover is valuable to it. It frequently crawls into the crocodile's mouth and cleans the huge reptile's teeth. The plover, in turn, gets a meal. The bird's job does not appear to endanger it, for the crocodiles never seem to harm the little feathered creatures. Both partners benefit from their curious but necessary relationship.

Main Idea   1

	Answer	Score
Mark the *main idea* ⟶	M	15
Mark the statement that is *too broad* ⟶	B	5
Mark the statement that is *too narrow* ⟶	N	5

a. In a symbiotic relationship, two different kinds of organisms help each other. ☐ _____

b. Living creatures help each other in a variety of ways. ☐ _____

c. Egrets and rhinos have a symbiotic relationship. ☐ _____

Score 15 points for each correct answer.   **Score**

Subject Matter

2 Another appropriate title for this passage might be

☐ a. Unusual Partners in Nature.
☐ b. Birds of Africa.
☐ c. The Origins of Symbiotic Partnerships.
☐ d. Enemies in Nature.   _____

Supporting Details

3 The crocodile provides

☐ a. a resting place for the plover.
☐ b. transportation for birds.
☐ c. a hiding place for the plover.
☐ d. food for the plover.   _____

Conclusion

4 It could be concluded from this passage that rhinoceroses

☐ a. are frightened by egrets.
☐ b. don't harm their egret partners.
☐ c. never participate in a symbiosis.
☐ d. are gentle animals.   _____

Clarifying Devices

5 The writer explains the meaning of symbiosis by giving

☐ a. examples only.
☐ b. a definition only.
☐ c. both a definition and examples.
☐ d. several synonyms.   _____

Vocabulary in Context

6 Confidently means

☐ a. fearfully.
☐ b. with assurance.
☐ c. precariously.
☐ d. happily.   _____

Add your scores for questions 1-6. Enter the total here and on the graph on page 238.   **Total Score** ☐

66

Champlain's Choice of Friends

Samuel de Champlain was one of the greatest French explorers of the New World. Early in his pioneering, Champlain made a choice of <u>allies</u> that was to have a tremendous influence on the course of history in North America.

Soon after landing on the North American coast, Champlain became friends with the Algonquin Indians. He and his men carried on their explorations of the wilderness in safety, accompanied by an Algonquin war party. Together they traveled hundreds of miles in large canoes, throughout Canada and the northern United States. While exploring the area surrounding what was eventually called Lake Champlain, they were confronted by members of the Iroquois Indian tribe, rivals of the Algonquin. The Iroquois had never seen white people. When they spotted Champlain coming forward with their enemies, they halted in astonishment. When Champlain and his men opened fire upon them, the Iroquois quickly retreated, while the Algonquin warriors rejoiced.

Although he didn't realize it, Champlain had started a bitter and bloody war that would last a hundred years. The Iroquois, a fierce and powerful people, never forgave the French for aiding the Algonquin. The Iroquois remained the most bitter enemies of France in the New World, and later gladly helped the English drive the French from the Canadian shores.

Main Idea	1		Answer	Score
		Mark the *main idea* ⟶	M	15
		Mark the statement that is *too broad* ⟶	B	5
		Mark the statement that is *too narrow* ⟶	N	5

a. Without realizing what he was doing, Champlain made the Iroquois enemies of the French. ☐ _____

b. Samuel de Champlain was a great explorer. ☐ _____

c. Champlain befriended the Algonquin Indians. ☐ _____

Score 15 points for each correct answer.   **Score**

Subject
Matter

2 The best alternate title for this passage would be

☐ a. The Fierce Iroquois.

☐ b. Indian Tribes of North America.

☐ c. Champlain and the Indians.

☐ d. Champlain's Explorations.   _____

Supporting
Details

3 The Algonquin

☐ a. were friends of the Iroquois.

☐ b. named Lake Champlain.

☐ c. were friends of the English.

☐ d. traveled with Champlain.   _____

Conclusion

4 The passage suggests that

☐ a. one shouldn't make friends with Indians.

☐ b. Champlain wasn't very good at choosing his friends.

☐ c. choices may have unforeseen results.

☐ d. the Algonquin let the French down.   _____

Clarifying
Devices

5 The method in which the passage is presented is primarily

☐ a. argument.

☐ b. analogy.

☐ c. narrative.

☐ d. questioning.   _____

Vocabulary
in Context

6 The best definition for the word <u>allies</u> is

☐ a. enemies.

☐ b. guides.

☐ c. warriors.

☐ d. friends.   _____

Add your scores for questions 1–6. Enter the total here and on the graph on page 238.   Total Score ☐

67

Queen of the Nile

Legend has made Cleopatra one of the world's best-known women and has created an image of her which is both incomplete and greatly <u>embellished.</u> Thanks to Shakespeare and other writers, she is thought of as a dark Egyptian seductress and pursuer of powerful men, a woman who was ruled by passion to such an extent that she killed herself over the death of her lover, Marc Antony. The truth? Well, to begin with, Cleopatra was blond, not dark, and despite the fact that she ruled Egypt, she was actually Greek.

Examination of the historical record doesn't support the notion that Cleopatra pursued men to any great extent. In fact, there is no evidence connecting her to any men other than, first, Julius Caesar and, then Marc Antony. Her relationship with Antony did not begin until four years after Caesar's death. Both unions were recognized in Egypt as marriages, and she was apparently a faithful and helpful wife to both men.

Much has been made of the "Queen of the Nile's" beauty, yet one contemporary observer wrote that her looks were far from remarkable. Her passionate nature has also been overemphasized. But her impressive knowledge of languages and skill in military strategy and political negotiations have been either ignored or forgotten.

Then there is the belief that Cleopatra killed herself for love. The truth is that she coolly ended her life in order to avoid humiliation and execution at the hands of Egypt's conqueror, Augustus Caesar.

Main Idea	1		Answer	Score
	Mark the *main idea* ⟶	M		15
	Mark the statement that is *too broad* ⟶	B		5
	Mark the statement that is *too narrow* ⟶	N		5
	a. There are a great many misconceptions about the legendary Cleopatra.	☐		___
	b. Cleopatra knew many languages and was skilled in military and political strategy.	☐		___
	c. Legend often distorts the images of historical figures.	☐		___

Subject Matter **2** The best alternate title for this passage would be

☐ a. The Beauty of Cleopatra.

☐ b. Cleopatra's Roman Marriages.

☐ c. The Truth About the Queen of the Nile.

☐ d. A Legendary Woman.   _____

Supporting Details **3** According to the passage, it is <u>not</u> true that Cleopatra was

☐ a. married twice.

☐ b. an Egyptian.

☐ c. politically skillful.

☐ d. a Greek.   _____

Conclusion **4** We can infer that Cleopatra

☐ a. didn't really rule Egypt, because she was Greek.

☐ b. allowed Caesar and Antony to rule for her.

☐ c. was an incompetent ruler.

☐ d. took an active role in political and military affairs.   _____

Clarifying Devices **5** In the second paragraph, *first* and *then* are used to indicate

☐ a. an important spatial relationship.

☐ b. emphasis on particular points.

☐ c. the order of events.

☐ d. the relative importance of two items.   _____

Vocabulary in Context **6** <u>Embellished</u> means

☐ a. having exaggerated characteristics.

☐ b. filled with interesting but untrue details.

☐ c. filled with deliberate lies.

☐ d. changed according to the whims of historians.   _____

Add your scores for questions 1–6. Enter the total here and on the graph on page 238.

Total Score ☐

68

The Great Battle for Quebec

For three months, the English general James Wolfe had attacked the French forces defending the city of Quebec, in Canada. Quebec is located on the banks of the mighty St. Lawrence River, and it controlled the shipping on this broad waterway that leads to the Great Lakes and the heart of the North American continent. France and Great Britain were competing for control of the American colonies in the Seven Years War of 1756–1763, and the key to an English victory was the conquest of Quebec and access to the St. Lawrence.

In a final desperate attempt, Wolfe decided to circle around the French forces and attack them from the rear. To do this, he had to cross the river, defeat a small group of French guards without allowing them to alarm the French troops, and then get his army of 4,000 men, with their weapons and equipment, up the cliffs known as the Plains of Abraham—all in a single dark night.

On September 13, 1759, the sun rose on an English army that had seemingly miraculously relocated itself to the rear of the French forces. A fierce battle followed, ending with both Wolfe and the French commander, Montcalm, dead on the field. But Wolfe's departing words, as the outcome of the battle became apparent, were "I die contented." While Montcalm, when he realized he was dying, cried, "Thank God I shall not live to see the surrender of Quebec."

Main Idea	1		Answer	Score
	Mark the *main idea*	→	M	15
	Mark the statement that is *too broad*	→	B	5
	Mark the statement that is *too narrow*	→	N	5

a. Both France and England wanted the American colonies. ☐ ____

b. General Wolfe attacked the French army that was defending Quebec. ☐ ____

c. The English won the battle for Quebec, which was the decisive battle of the Seven Years War. ☐ ____

Score 15 points for each correct answer. Score

Subject Matter

2 This passage focuses on
- [ ] a. two great generals.
- [ ] b. the Seven Years War of 1756–1763.
- [ ] c. the battle for Quebec.
- [ ] d. the Plains of Abraham. _____

Supporting Details

3 According to the passage, Wolfe was
- [ ] a. cool and collected.
- [ ] b. anxious to conquer Quebec.
- [ ] c. apathetic to the war's cause.
- [ ] d. not a very good general. _____

Conclusion

4 We can infer from the passage that
- [ ] a. this battle had no effect on the American colonies.
- [ ] b. Wolfe's plan was successful.
- [ ] c. Montcalm was a bad general.
- [ ] d. the sun's position suddenly changed. _____

Clarifying Devices

5 The writer reveals the result of the battle by
- [ ] a. quoting the last words of the opposing commanders.
- [ ] b. implying that God was on the side of the English.
- [ ] c. presenting the entire passage from the English point of view.
- [ ] d. relying on the reader's knowledge of history. _____

Vocabulary in Context

6 In this passage, the word key means
- [ ] a. a device for opening a lock.
- [ ] b. essential element.
- [ ] c. a musical pitch.
- [ ] d. a legend on a map. _____

Add your scores for questions 1–6. Enter the total here and on the graph on page 238.

Total Score [____]

69

Insects for Dinner

Most Americans seem to like variety in their diets, judging by the popularity of foreign food restaurants. But though many people would be willing to try a rice and fish dish from China, or a real Hungarian goulash, very few would want to sample a kind of food that is popular in many countries: insects.

Eating insects actually makes a lot of sense. There are certainly enough of them around, and though most are too small to bother with, many grow to a <u>respectable</u> size or live in dense groups that can be easily harvested. They are very nutritious, for, after all, many birds and mammals eat nothing but insects. And since they contain a fair amount of salt, they are already well seasoned. Indeed, in those countries where insects are eaten, they are usually considered great delicacies. The goliath beetle is a prize catch in Africa, caterpillars are a popular dish in Mexico, where they are fried and served under the name of "agave worms," and chocolate-covered bees and ants are favorite candies in Switzerland.

It is unlikely that canned grasshoppers will become popular in America in the near future but who knows? Perhaps in years to come people will rid themselves of their prejudice against insects and will find themselves going out to dig for grubs as eagerly as others go out to gather mushrooms.

Main Idea	1		Answer	Score
	Mark the *main idea* ⟶		M	15
	Mark the statement that is *too broad* ⟶		B	5
	Mark the statement that is *too narrow* ⟶		N	5
	a. Insects contain a fair amount of salt.	☐		___
	b. Many different creatures are edible.	☐		___
	c. Insects can be a good source of food.	☐		___

Score 15 points for each correct answer. **Score**

Subject Matter

2 The subject of this passage is
- ☐ a. how to open a restaurant.
- ☐ b. the behavior of primitive people.
- ☐ c. American shopping habits.
- ☐ d. the use of insects as food. _____

Supporting Details

3 Agave worms are
- ☐ a. caterpillars found in Mexico.
- ☐ b. fried vegetables.
- ☐ c. pests found on agave trees.
- ☐ d. salty and very crunchy. _____

Conclusion

4 This passage implies that insects are not a popular food in America because
- ☐ a. they can transmit deadly diseases.
- ☐ b. Americans don't like salty food.
- ☐ c. Americans don't like the idea of eating such creatures.
- ☐ d. very few restaurants offer them. _____

Clarifying Devices

5 In developing the idea that insects are good to eat, the author uses
- ☐ a. an emotional appeal.
- ☐ b. several specific examples.
- ☐ c. the opinions of some famous people.
- ☐ d. only broad generalizations. _____

Vocabulary in Context

6 In this passage respectable means
- ☐ a. awesome.
- ☐ b. well-behaved.
- ☐ c. fairly large.
- ☐ d. dangerous. _____

Add your scores for questions 1-6. Enter the total here and on the graph on page 238. **Total Score** ☐

Dangerous to Your Health

"Warning: The surgeon general has determined that cigarette smoking is dangerous to your health." When you see this statement, what do you think of? The 1964 surgeon general's report established cigarette smoking as a primary cause of lung cancer, and, since then, most Americans have mentally connected the two.

But suppose a cigarette smoker regularly has his or her lungs examined and everything seems fine? Or what if a pipe or cigar smoker doesn't inhale? Doesn't this mean they have no smoke-related health worries? The answer is a definite "no."

In addition to the obvious dangers of lung cancer and other respiratory ailments, smoking has been associated with higher rates of many other kinds of health problems that are less well known. For example, the pipe or cigar smoker runs a greater risk of contracting cancer of the lips, mouth and larynx.

Much evidence suggests that women should be concerned about smoking during pregnancy. Women who smoke generally give birth to babies who weigh less. There is also a greater probability that the mother will have a spontaneous abortion, a premature delivery, or a stillbirth.

Although it is not generally recognized, smoking is the leading cause of peptic ulcers and has been linked to gum disease, tooth loss and even sinusitis. Amblyopia, a condition that causes a person's sight to grow progressively dimmer, is also directly linked to excessive smoking.

Main Idea 1

	Answer	Score
Mark the *main idea* →	M	15
Mark the statement that is *too broad* →	B	5
Mark the statement that is *too narrow* →	N	5
a. Pregnant women who smoke risk harming their unborn children.	☐	
b. Smoking can cause many health problems in addition to lung cancer.	☐	
c. Smoking is a bad habit many people engage in.	☐	

Score 15 points for each correct answer.   **Score**

Subject Matter

2 This passage is mostly about

☐ a. how smoking causes lung cancer.

☐ b. the health problems associated with smoking.

☐ c. why people smoke.

☐ d. how smoking affects pregnant women.   _____

Supporting Details

3 The 1964 surgeon general's report

☐ a. showed that pregnant women shouldn't smoke.

☐ b. claimed that smoking is a leading cause of peptic ulcers.

☐ c. has not been taken seriously by the general public.

☐ d. said that smoking is a major cause of lung cancer.   _____

Conclusion

4 This passage implies that

☐ a. smokers should not be concerned about the dangers of lung cancer.

☐ b. the general public has been misled about the dangers of smoking.

☐ c. many people are unaware of the many and varied dangers of smoking.

☐ d. people who smoke run a high risk of going blind.   _____

Clarifying Devices

5 To develop the main idea, the author uses mainly

☐ a. factual information.

☐ b. an emotional appeal.

☐ c. a narrative description.

☐ d. statistical evidence.   _____

Vocabulary in Context

6 In this passage, <u>primary</u> means

☐ a. leading.

☐ b. first.

☐ c. early grades.

☐ d. dangerous.   _____

Add your scores for questions 1–6. Enter the total here and on the graph on page 238.   **Total Score** ☐

71

Who's Superstitious?

Many people who achieved great things were superstitious. For example, did you know that Napoleon, the great French general who won countless battles, was afraid of cats? People tend to believe that superstition is linked to ignorance, but this is not entirely true.

Many brilliant people have been superstitious. Rousseau, the famous French philosopher, believed he had a ghost for a companion. William Blake, an English writer and painter, thought he was a brother to Socrates, who had died in 399 B.C.! And Sir Walter Scott would never go to Melrose Abbey when the full moon shone brightly.

Superstitions usually arise when people try to find reasons for things that are beyond their understanding. Primitive societies created all kinds of fantastic explanations for illness, death and natural events. People looked and wondered at the sky, and developed wonderful stories to account for the various clusters of stars.

Even the age of science has not destroyed people's beliefs in irrational things. The following story is a good example. A panic shook Europe when Halley's comet was expected to appear in 1910. It seemed that whenever this comet had appeared in the past, devastating events had taken place. In A.D. 66, for example, its appearance coincided with the fall of Jerusalem. So, the people of the twentieth century feared another catastrophe. They were so frightened that they even bought anti-comet pills and masks to protect themselves from deadly fumes.

Main Idea   1

	Answer	Score
Mark the *main idea* ⟶	**M**	15
Mark the statement that is *too broad* ⟶	**B**	5
Mark the statement that is *too narrow* ⟶	**N**	5

a. Even many intelligent people are superstitious. ☐ _____

b. Most people are superstitious. ☐ _____

c. Napoleon, who was highly intelligent, was afraid of cats. ☐ _____

Subject Matter

2 Another good title for this story would be

☐ a. Fear of Black Cats.

☐ b. Napoleon the General.

☐ c. Superstition and Intelligence.

☐ d. Panic in Europe.

_____

Supporting Details

3 William Blake was

☐ a. Napoleon's friend.

☐ b. a French philosopher.

☐ c. an English writer.

☐ d. a brother to Socrates.

_____

Conclusion

4 This passage suggests that

☐ a. superstitious people are not always ignorant.

☐ b. anti-comet pills are effective.

☐ c. people panic too easily.

☐ d. Socrates was a brilliant Greek philosopher.

_____

Clarifying Devices

5 The writer develops the main idea primarily through the use of

☐ a. descriptions.

☐ b. historical examples.

☐ c. comparisons.

☐ d. anecdotes.

_____

Vocabulary in Context

6 As used in this passage, the word <u>irrational</u> means

☐ a. silly.

☐ b. beyond reason.

☐ c. unimportant.

☐ d. general.

_____

Add your scores for questions 1-6. Enter the total here and on the graph on page 238.

Total Score ☐

72

Indians Laugh, Too!

The American Indian is frequently featured as a shrewd and fierce warrior. However, the Indian is seldom credited with having the original American sense of humor.

Indians actually laughed more than they fought. Many of them loved to pull pranks or tell their favorite stories, the most popular of which involved puns and hilarious exaggerations. The normally stern faced Indians could be reduced to tears of laughter by a good joke. The jokes themselves were usually clever and <u>dry</u>, and not easily appreciated by the uninitiated. Indians often joked about their dreams. In fact, dreams that dealt with exaggerated personal experiences were the mainstay of Indian humor.

As with many aspects of Indian life, joke telling was not without its rules and limitations. The careless brave who cracked a joke to his mother-in-law soon learned that this kind of behavior was expressly forbidden. Similarly, as a gesture of respect, wisecracking young tribes-men did not joke with the elderly men of the tribe.

Jokes told to relative strangers were told with caution. Usually the joke teller would follow his jest with a crack about himself. Sometimes the comedian would offer a present to the victim of his humor. Even in comedy, Indians valued tradition.

Main Idea 1

	Answer	Score
Mark the *main idea* →	M	15
Mark the statement that is *too broad* →	B	5
Mark the statement that is *too narrow* →	N	5

a. The American Indians liked to be entertained. ☐ ____

b. Indian jokes often involved dreams. ☐ ____

c. The American Indians enjoyed jokes and had good senses of humor. ☐ ____

Score 15 points for each correct answer. **Score**

Subject Matter

2 This passage is about

- ☐ a. Indian cuisine.
- ☐ b. Indian war strategy.
- ☐ c. Indian humor.
- ☐ d. Indian theater.

_____

Supporting Details

3 Indians never joked with their

- ☐ a. children.
- ☐ b. parents.
- ☐ c. stepfathers.
- ☐ d. mothers-in-law.

_____

Conclusion

4 One might conclude from this passage that

- ☐ a. Indians never smile.
- ☐ b. Indians enjoyed laughing.
- ☐ c. Indian jokes were silly.
- ☐ d. older Indians had no sense of humor.

_____

Clarifying Devices

5 The first paragraph contrasts Indian

- ☐ a. humor and government.
- ☐ b. customs and religion.
- ☐ c. philosophy and religion.
- ☐ d. humor and ferocity.

_____

Vocabulary in Context

6 In this passage <u>dry</u> means

- ☐ a. lacking moisture.
- ☐ b. lacking interest.
- ☐ c. lacking expression.
- ☐ d. lacking alcohol.

_____

Add your scores for questions 1-6. Enter the total here and on the graph on page 238.

Total Score ☐

73

A Mystery Solved

During the 1950s, Peter Glob, a Danish archaeologist, solved the mystery of a centuries-old murder.

Several well-preserved, naked male bodies were discovered in Danish peat bogs. Upon examining these bodies, Glob found that they dated back to Denmark's Iron Age, more than 1,600 years ago. The apparent fact that the men had died violently, by hanging or throat slitting, was the first clue to intrigue Glob. Several victims wore twisted hide thongs around their necks, and their hands and feet were soft, indicating that they had never done heavy labor. Autopsies revealed that the men's last meal consisted of grains and seeds. Glob found the absence of meat puzzling, because during the Iron Age people were not vegetarians.

In search of further information, Glob turned to the writings of Tacitus, the ancient Roman historian who had written about the tribes of northwest Europe. Tacitus described rites of human sacrifice that were made to the Earth Goddess. The ancient tribes held these rites in early spring, to guarantee the fertility of their fields. From this information, Glob deduced that the dead men were priests or men of high rank, which would account for their soft hands, and that the victims had been fed a ritual meal of plant seeds before they were sacrificed. Glob further deduced that the victims' leather neck thongs represented the metal ring which Tacitus described as being a symbol for the Earth Goddess. Glob concluded that these bog men had been sacrificed to the very thing that preserved them—Mother Earth.

Main Idea	1		Answer	Score
	Mark the *main idea* ———————→	M		15
	Mark the statement that is *too broad* ———→	B		5
	Mark the statement that is *too narrow* ———→	N		5

a. The preserved bodies of men who lived in Denmark 1,600 years ago were found to have been sacrificed to the Earth Goddess. ☐ _____

b. A Danish archaeologist solved the mystery of the men in the bog. ☐ _____

c. Archaeologists uncover many mysterious things in the course of their work. ☐ _____

Score 15 points for each correct answer.   **Score**

Subject Matter

2 Which would be the best alternate title for this passage?

☐ a. Tribes of Northwest Europe
☐ b. Peter Glob, Danish Archaeologist
☐ c. Identifying the Bodies in the Bog
☐ d. Murder in Ancient Europe   _____

Supporting Details

3 According to the passage, the dead men's bodies were

☐ a. decomposed.
☐ b. tied together.
☐ c. well-preserved.
☐ d. cut into pieces.   _____

Conclusion

4 We can conclude from the passage that the key information linking the men in the bog to ancient human sacrifices was provided by

☐ a. autopsies of the bodies.
☐ b. the writings of Tacitus.
☐ c. the examination of the victims' hands and feet.
☐ d. the positions of the bodies.   _____

Clarifying Devices

5 The writer's purpose in the first sentence is to

☐ a. mislead the reader.
☐ b. provide important information.
☐ c. arouse the reader's interest.
☐ d. scare the reader.   _____

Vocabulary in Context

6 As used in the passage, the word <u>intrigue</u> means

☐ a. maneuver.
☐ b. frighten.
☐ c. greatly interest.
☐ d. mislead.   _____

Add your scores for questions 1-6. Enter the total here and on the graph on page 238.   **Total Score** ☐

74

Nature's Gigantic Snowplow

On January 10, 1962, an enormous piece of a glacier broke away and tumbled down the side of a mountain in Peru. A mere seven minutes later, when the cascading ice finally came to a stop ten miles down the mountain, it had taken the lives of 4,000 people.

This disaster is one of the most <u>devastating</u> examples of a very common event: an avalanche of snow or ice. Because it is extremely cold at very high altitudes, snow rarely melts. It just keeps piling up higher and higher. Glaciers are eventually created, when the weight of the snow is so great that the lower layers are pressed into solid ice. But most avalanches occur long before this happens. As snow accumulates on a steep slope, it reaches a critical point at which the slightest vibration will send it sliding into the valley below.

Even an avalanche of light powder can be dangerous, but the Peruvian catastrophe was particularly terrible because it was caused by a heavy layer of ice. It is estimated that the ice that broke off weighed three million tons. As it crashed down the steep mountainside like a gigantic snowplow, it swept up trees, boulders and tons of topsoil, and completely crushed and destroyed the six villages that lay in its path.

At present there is no way to predict or avoid such enormous avalanches, but, luckily, they are very rare. Scientists are constantly studying the smaller, more common avalanches, to try to understand what causes them. In the future, perhaps dangerous masses of snow or ice can be found and removed before they take human lives.

Main Idea	1		Answer	Score
		Mark the *main idea* ⟶	M	15
		Mark the statement that is *too broad* ⟶	B	5
		Mark the statement that is *too narrow* ⟶	N	5
		a. Avalanches of snow or ice can be very dangerous and unpredictable.	☐	____
		b. There are many hazards to living in the mountains.	☐	____
		c. Thousands of people died in an avalanche in Peru in 1962.	☐	____

Score 15 points for each correct answer.   **Score**

Subject
Matter

2 This passage is mostly about

☐ a. Peru.
☐ b. glaciers.
☐ c. avalanches.
☐ d. mountains.   _____

Supporting
Details

3 The Peruvian avalanche described in this
passage was started by

☐ a. snow.
☐ b. ice.
☐ c. mud.
☐ d. water.   _____

Conclusion

4 You can assume that an avalanche is most
likely to occur

☐ a. after a heavy snowfall.
☐ b. on mountain peaks.
☐ c. during the night.
☐ d. when there is a strong wind.   _____

Clarifying
Devices

5 The first paragraph catches the reader's
attention with a

☐ a. first-hand story.
☐ b. dramatic story.
☐ c. tall tale.
☐ d. vivid word picture.   _____

Vocabulary
in Context

6 In this passage <u>devastating</u> means

☐ a. stunning.
☐ b. spectacularly interesting.
☐ c. unpleasant.
☐ d. violently ruinous.   _____

Add your scores for questions 1-6. Enter the   **Total** ☐
total here and on the graph on page 238.   **Score**

75

Identity Crisis

If you have ever been mistaken for somebody else, you can certainly sympathize with two young women from Maryland, both named Wanda Marie Johnson.

One Wanda was living and working in Washington, D.C., when she became confused with the second Wanda, a former resident of the area, whom she'd never met. Both Wandas were born on June 15, 1953, and their social security numbers are the same except for the final three digits. Amazingly, they both moved from Washington to St. George's, Grenada.

Both women drove cars of the same year and model, which really confused the computers at the Department of Motor Vehicles. When one of the Wandas applied for her driver's license, she was told she already had one and that she was required to wear glasses while driving. She spoke to four supervisors before convincing the authorities that her vision was perfect and that she really did need a license. She then received two licenses instead of one.

The Wandas also became confused in medical and credit records. One of the women was hounded for not paying a bill for furniture she had never purchased. She couldn't convince a skeptical debt collector that she'd never been in the store.

Newspapers finally picked up the story, and the identity confusion was brought to light. The Wandas met to discuss solutions to their bizarre predicament. One Wanda was reported to be considering using her maiden name.

Main Idea	1		Answer	Score
	Mark the *main idea* ⟶		M	15
	Mark the statement that is *too broad* ⟶		B	5
	Mark the statement that is *too narrow* ⟶		N	5

a. Two women with the same name and an amazing number of other coincidental similarities were often confused with one another. ☐ _____

b. There were two Wanda Marie Johnsons in the Washington, D.C. area. ☐ _____

c. People with the same name are often confused with one another. ☐ _____

Subject Matter

2 Another good title for the passage would be

☐ a. Common Names.

☐ b. Computer Mix-ups.

☐ c. Coincidence Causes Confusion.

☐ d. Dealing With the Department of Motor Vehicles.   _____

Supporting Details

3 According to the article, all of the following are true about the two Wandas except that

☐ a. they both lived in St. George's, Grenada.

☐ b. they both wore glasses.

☐ c. they had the same birthday.

☐ d. they drove the same type of car.   _____

Conclusion

4 The passage implies that

☐ a. computers caused the problem for the two Wandas.

☐ b. the only similarity between the two women was their name.

☐ c. the newspapers helped solve the problem for the two Wandas.

☐ d. the women's problems were solved when one moved to Grenada.   _____

Clarifying Devices

5 In the passage, the writer frequently uses

☐ a. vivid adjectives and adverbs.

☐ b. logically reasoned arguments.

☐ c. pointed accusations.

☐ d. factual detail.   _____

Vocabulary in Context

6 The word skeptical is closest in meaning to

☐ a. free-thinking.

☐ b. cruel.

☐ c. doubting.

☐ d. incompetent.   _____

Add your scores for questions 1–6. Enter the total here and on the graph on page 238.   Total Score ☐

76

The Charge of O'Higgins's Brigade

The country of Chile can credit its independence to the military expertise of a herd of sheep, cows, mules and dogs—thanks to the brilliant plan of Bernardo O'Higgins, Chile's first ruler.

In 1814, Bernardo O'Higgins was the renegade leader of a small group of Chileans who were rebelling against their Spanish rulers. The Spanish outnumbered the courageous patriots and slowly but surely drove the Chileans into retreat. By October 1814, the Spanish had successfully surrounded O'Higgins and his weary followers. When O'Higgins was wounded in battle, morale dropped drastically. Only a miracle could have saved the surrounded band. And O'Higgins arranged for one.

He had his soldiers round up all the farm animals in the area. He then arranged his soldiers directly behind the confused ranks of the animal army. Suddenly O'Higgins gave the order to charge. The noise, the shouting and the firing of weapons panicked the animals, and they stampeded wildly toward the Spanish lines.

The battle-hardened Spanish army was not easily frightened, but the sight of hundreds of stampeding beasts was too much for them. The Spanish lines broke in wild confusion.

O'Higgins and his men charged through the gap in the enemy lines and were safely in the hills before the Spanish recovered from the shock. Their escape provided the patriots with the chance to regroup. Bernardo O'Higgins returned to battle and defeated the Spanish in 1818.

Main Idea   1

	Answer	Score
Mark the *main idea* ⟶	M	15
Mark the statement that is *too broad* ⟶	B	5
Mark the statement that is *too narrow* ⟶	N	5

a. Bernardo O'Higgins was the leader of a group of Chilean patriots. ☐ ____

b. Creative thinking can help people win battles against strong odds. ☐ ____

c. Bernardo O'Higgins helped Chile gain its independence by using a bunch of farm animals to win an important battle. ☐ ____

Score 15 points for each correct answer.   **Score**

Subject Matter **2** The subject of this passage is

☐ a. the Spanish-American War.

☐ b. Spanish conquests in South America.

☐ c. how farm animals helped Chile gain its independence.

☐ d. the plight of the Spanish army.   _____

Supporting Details **3** The Chilean patriots were at a disadvantage because they were

☐ a. poor soldiers.

☐ b. outnumbered.

☐ c. on unfamiliar ground.

☐ d. short of horses.   _____

Conclusion **4** One could conclude from this passage that Bernardo O'Higgins was

☐ a. a paid fighter.

☐ b. a trained general.

☐ c. a native Chilean.

☐ d. an imaginative man.   _____

Clarifying Devices **5** The writer

☐ a. tells a fable.

☐ b. gives a historical account.

☐ c. gives an eyewitness account.

☐ d. thinks O'Higgins was lucky.   _____

Vocabulary in Context **6** In this passage <u>band</u> means

☐ a. a musical group.

☐ b. a group of people.

☐ c. a thin ring.

☐ d. a song on a record.   _____

Add your scores for questions 1–6. Enter the total here and on the graph on page 238.   **Total Score** ☐

77

The Mad Emperor

Recently, a group of historians from all over the world announced its list of the ten greatest tyrants of all time. The unanimous choice for number one tyrant was Nero, the third century Roman emperor.

The deranged ruler may have picked up many of his sadistic tendencies from his immediate ancestors. His widowed mother Agrippina, was the sister of Caligula, the gleeful and insane ruler who tortured and murdered hundreds of Romans. Agrippina married the emperor Claudius. She convinced him to disinherit his natural son, Brittannicus, and make Nero his successor. She then <u>served</u> Claudius poison mushrooms before he could change his mind.

Nero's tyranny was most brutally expressed in his treatment of his own family. Upon ascending the throne at the age of sixteen, he committed his first recorded murder. He gave his rival, Brittannicus, a fatal potion to drink during a meal. The other guests were alarmed at the youth's death spasms, but Nero called it "an epileptic fit" and calmly went back to eating.

Then Nero dealt with his mother. After she started meddling in governmental matters, he sent her out for a sail in a sabotaged boat. When she survived her ordeal, Nero had her executed.

Nero's marriages also reflected his bloodthirsty personality. His first marriage, to his thirteen-year-old stepsister, ended when he had her banished and then murdered. He killed his second wife when she scolded him for coming home late. He obtained his third and final wife by having her husband eliminated.

Main Idea	1		Answer	Score
	Mark the *main idea* →		M	15
	Mark the statement that is *too broad* →		B	5
	Mark the statement that is *too narrow* →		N	5
	a. Nero was a tyrant and a cold-blooded murderer who ruthlessly killed his own relatives.		☐	____
	b. Nero's family background seems to contain the seeds of his bloodthirsty personality.		☐	____
	c. Throughout history, there have been rulers who were tyrants and murderers.		☐	____

Subject Matter **2** The passage is primarily about

☐ a. Nero's family background.

☐ b. Nero's mother, Agrippina.

☐ c. history's greatest tyrants.

☐ d. Nero as a callous murderer.   _____

Supporting Details **3** It could be said that Nero followed his mother's example in all of the following <u>except</u>

☐ a. killing a spouse.

☐ b. poisoning a family member.

☐ c. murdering to secure his place as emperor.

☐ d. killing a brother.   _____

Conclusion **4** The passage implies that Nero murdered Britannicus because

☐ a. they did not have the same political views.

☐ b. Agrippina supported Britannicus's claim to the throne.

☐ c. Britannicus was a rival for Nero's wife.

☐ d. Nero feared that Britannicus would attempt to reclaim the throne.   _____

Clarifying Devices **5** The writer mentions the historians' naming Nero as a great tyrant in order to

☐ a. point out that this reputation is not deserved.

☐ b. contrast Nero's personality with Agrippina's.

☐ c. give authority to the portrait of Nero as a brutal person.

☐ d. compare Nero with other tyrants.   _____

Vocabulary in Context **6** In this passage <u>served</u> means

☐ a. hit the ball, as in tennis.

☐ b. loyally obeyed.

☐ c. gave to eat.

☐ d. waited out.   _____

Add your scores for questions 1–6. Enter the total here and on the graph on page 238.   **Total Score** ☐

78

The Deadly Nuisance

D.H. Lawrence assailed it as "that small, high, hateful bugle." What is it? The mosquito. Most of us think of her—only the females bite—as just a summertime nuisance. We barricade ourselves behind screens, invest in insect repellent, and, finally, apply lotions when we inevitably get bitten. But for centuries the mosquito has been recognized as more than an inconvenience. It is a carrier of some of the deadliest diseases.

As a disease carrier, the mosquito has been most frequently associated with the fever and chills of malaria. Although the United States and most developed nations have now either eradicated or significantly controlled this disease, malaria still afflicts more than 150 million people in the tropics, killing more than a million children a year in Africa alone.

Yellow fever is another disease carried by mosquitoes. It has been brought under control in North America, so we tend to think of it as an exotic disease. But, though it is now confined to Africa and South America, it retains its deadly power.

Encephalitis, which can cause brain damage or death, is the one mosquito-borne human disease that still appears in the U.S. Common birds carry this disease too, but it's the pesky mosquito that transmits it to people. Most of the time, your risk of contracting encephalitis is <u>minimal</u>, but the chances increase when the mosquito population swells. So remember, screens and insect repellent may be protection from much more than a mere nuisance.

			Answer	Score
Main Idea	1			
		Mark the *main idea* →	M	15
		Mark the statement that is *too broad* →	B	5
		Mark the statement that is *too narrow* →	N	5
		a. Mosquitoes are carriers of deadly diseases, in addition to being pests.	☐	_____
		b. People tend to think of the mosquito as a simple nuisance.	☐	_____
		c. Many animals and insects transmit diseases to humans.	☐	_____

Score 15 points for each correct answer. **Score**

Subject Matter

2 This passage is primarily about
- [ ] a. the causes of malaria and yellow fever.
- [ ] b. how mosquitoes bite their victims.
- [ ] c. diseases carried by insects.
- [ ] d. the mosquito's function as a disease carrier. _____

Supporting Details

3 According to the passage, people in the U.S. still have a chance of contracting
- [ ] a. yellow fever.
- [ ] b. encephalitis.
- [ ] c. malaria.
- [ ] d. filariasis. _____

Conclusion

4 The final sentence of the passage implies that the writer thinks
- [ ] a. disease-carrying mosquitoes still pose a significant threat.
- [ ] b. screens and insect repellent are ineffective protection against mosquitoes.
- [ ] c. the threat of disease being transmitted by mosquitoes no longer exists in the U.S.
- [ ] d. screens and insect repellent are the best protection against mosquitoes. _____

Clarifying Devices

5 The writer quotes D.H. Lawrence's description of the mosquito to
- [ ] a. help the reader visualize the insect's appearance.
- [ ] b. convey factual information.
- [ ] c. catch the reader's attention.
- [ ] d. contrast it with his own description. _____

Vocabulary in Context

6 The word <u>minimal</u> is closest in meaning to
- [ ] a. nonexistent.
- [ ] b. frightening.
- [ ] c. average.
- [ ] d. slight. _____

Add your scores for questions 1-6. Enter the total here and on the graph on page 238.

Total Score

79

A Greek to Remember

Diogenes was a famous Greek philosopher of the fourth century B.C., who established the philosophy of cynicism. He often walked about in the daytime holding a lighted lantern, peering around as if he were looking for something. When questioned about his odd behavior he would reply, "I am searching for an honest man."

Diogenes <u>held</u> that the good man was self-sufficient and did not require material comforts or wealth. He believed that wealth and possessions constrained humanity's natural state of freedom. In keeping with his philosophy, he was perfectly satisfied with making his home in a large tub discarded from the Temple of Cybele, the goddess of nature. This earthen tub, called a pithos, had formerly been used for holding wine or oil for the sacrifices at the temple.

One day, Alexander the Great, conqueror of half the civilized world, saw Diogenes sitting in his tub in the sunshine. So the king, surrounded by his courtiers, approached Diogenes and said, "I am Alexander the Great." The philosopher replied rather contemptuously, "I am Diogenes, the Cynic." Alexander then asked him if he could help him in any way. "Yes," shot back Diogenes, "don't stand between me and the sun." A surprised Alexander then replied quickly, "If I were not Alexander, I would be Diogenes."

Main Idea 1

	Answer	Score
Mark the *main idea* ⟶	**M**	15
Mark the statement that is *too broad* ⟶	**B**	5
Mark the statement that is *too narrow* ⟶	**N**	5

a. Diogenes was a Greek philosopher. ☐ _____

b. Diogenes believed in humanity's natural state of freedom, a state without material luxuries. ☐ _____

c. Diogenes was a famous Greek who strictly adhered to his philosophy of cynicism. ☐ _____

Score 15 points for each correct answer.   Score

Subject Matter

2 This passage is mainly about
☐ a. cynical behavior.
☐ b. a famous cynic.
☐ c. ancient philosophers.
☐ d. Alexander the Great.   _____

Supporting Details

3 According to Diogenes, material luxuries
☐ a. make people self-sufficient and independent.
☐ b. enslave people to a world of possessions.
☐ c. give people happiness and joy.
☐ d. cause people grief and pain.   _____

Conclusion

4 One can conclude that Diogenes's reply
☐ a. angered Alexander.
☐ b. confused Alexander.
☐ c. impressed Alexander.
☐ d. amazed Alexander.   _____

Clarifying Devices

5 The writer shows that Diogenes lived according to his beliefs by
☐ a. giving examples of things he did.
☐ b. using logical reasoning.
☐ c. comparing his life with the lives of other philosophers.
☐ d. contrasting his lifestyle with Alexander's. _____

Vocabulary in Context

6 Held, in this passage, means
☐ a. confirmed.
☐ b. refuted.
☐ c. believed.
☐ d. opposed.   _____

Add your scores for questions 1–6. Enter the total here and on the graph on page 238.   Total Score ☐

80

Living Twice

In 1952, an American housewife named Virginia Tighe was hypnotized and began to talk about her previous life as an Irish girl named Bridey Murphy. In 1956, a book called *The Search for Bridey Murphy* was written about her experience, and it became a best seller. Thousands of people believed that it gave solid evidence for reincarnation—the rebirth of the soul into another body. They flocked to hypnotists to find out what their <u>former</u> lives had been like.

Of course, not everyone immediately believed that Virginia Tighe had lived a previous life in Ireland. It was impressive that she spoke with an Irish accent when under hypnosis, but some people looked for further proof. They went all the way to Ireland to find the places she mentioned and to look for records of a girl named Bridey Murphy. They didn't find anything definite, but some people closer to home did—in Virginia's home town of Chicago, Illinois.

In Chicago, they found a woman whose maiden name had been Bridie Murphy, and who had lived across the street from Virginia. They found people who remembered that in high school Virginia had liked to talk with an Irish accent. When Virginia was a child, relatives had told her stories about things that had happened to them, and these stories were just like those remembered by "Bridey Murphy." In short, there was no evidence at all that Virginia remembered anything from a previous life—only things from her own childhood. Bridey Murphy was just a fantasy, popular with people who wanted a reason to believe in life after death.

Main Idea	1		Answer	Score
	Mark the *main idea* ⟶		M	15
	Mark the statement that is *too broad* ⟶		B	5
	Mark the statement that is *too narrow* ⟶		N	5

a. Virginia Tighe was believed to have lived a previous life as an Irish girl named Bridey Murphy. ☐ _____

b. Many people believe in reincarnation. ☐ _____

c. People who went to Ireland found no records of Bridey Murphy. ☐ _____

Subject Matter **2** This passage focuses on

☐ a. the uses of hypnotism.
☐ b. Irish immigrants.
☐ c. Virginia Tighe's story.
☐ d. a best-selling book. _____

Supporting Details **3** What is mentioned as one reason that people believed Virginia Tighe once lived in Ireland?

☐ a. Her relatives told stories about it.
☐ b. Her hair was red.
☐ c. Records were found in Chicago.
☐ d. She had an Irish accent when hypnotized. _____

Conclusion **4** The author suggests that the book *The Search for Bridey Murphy* became a best seller because

☐ a. it was a very well-written, exciting story.
☐ b. several churches recommended it as a true story.
☐ c. Bridey Murphy was a famous Irish saint.
☐ d. many people wanted to believe in reincarnation. _____

Clarifying Devices **5** To support the view that Bridey Murphy was a fantasy, the author uses

☐ a. humor and sarcasm.
☐ b. several facts.
☐ c. an emotional appeal.
☐ d. logical argument. _____

Vocabulary in Context **6** Which word could best be substituted for <u>former</u>?

☐ a. Previous
☐ b. Primitive
☐ c. Usual
☐ d. First _____

Add your scores for questions 1-6. Enter the total here and on the graph on page 238. Total Score ☐

81

The World's Bloodiest Acre

This site of splendor once housed a carnival of carnage. The Roman Colosseum has been hailed as a "vision of beauty." Michelangelo is said to have wandered there "to lift his soul." Many tourists still flock to see the majestic ruins. Built over 1,900 years ago, this amphitheater is often looked upon as a symbol of human artistry and intellect. But the history of what took place there reveals a dark side of human nature.

The Emperor Vespasian, who began the Colosseum's construction, did not live to see its completion, but his son, Titus, did. It was Titus who began the bloody "games" which were held in the great ring of the Colosseum for over 400 years. Ceremonies held by Titus to inaugurate the structure lasted for 100 days. In these, beast was <u>pitted</u> against beast, man against beast, and man against man, in battles to the death.

For the next three hundred years, a number of programs similar to, but more modest than Titus's, continued to be held at the Colosseum. Bloodthirsty spectators often clamored for "the game without end," a never-ending bout in which an armed man slaughtered a defenseless opponent. The victor of each contest was then disarmed and became the victim of another armed participant.

In A.D. 404, human contests were finally banned. But for still another century, animals were slaughtered in the Colosseum for the entertainment of the Roman populace. The impressive arena's gory history has prompted one writer to call it "The World's Bloodiest Acre."

Main Idea	1		Answer	Score
		Mark the *main idea* ⟶	**M**	15
		Mark the statement that is *too broad* ⟶	**B**	5
		Mark the statement that is *too narrow* ⟶	**N**	5

a. The Colosseum was the site of centuries of bloody forms of entertainment. ☐ _____

b. Society in ancient Rome enjoyed bloody pastimes. ☐ _____

c. After its completion, there was a gory 100-day celebration at the Colosseum. ☐ _____

Subject Matter

2 The passage is primarily about

- ☐ a. Emperor Titus's first 100 days as emperor.
- ☐ b. the construction of the Colosseum.
- ☐ c. the competitions held in the Colosseum.
- ☐ d. the beauty of the Colosseum.

———

Supporting Details

3 According to the passage, what entertainment was particularly popular with the Roman spectators?

- ☐ a. The slaughtering of animals
- ☐ b. Beast in competition against beast
- ☐ c. Man in competition against beast
- ☐ d. The game without end

———

Conclusion

4 The first paragraph of the passage implies that

- ☐ a. the Colosseum is not as beautiful as most people believe.
- ☐ b. tourists have destroyed the Colosseum.
- ☐ c. the passage of time has ruined the beauty of the Colosseum.
- ☐ d. the history of the Colosseum was not beautiful.

———

Clarifying Devices

5 The phrase "a dark side of human nature" refers to

- ☐ a. ancient human accomplishments.
- ☐ b. human history during the Dark Ages.
- ☐ c. human cruelty.
- ☐ d. ancient human competition.

———

Vocabulary in Context

6 In this passage pitted means

- ☐ a. full of dents.
- ☐ b. set against.
- ☐ c. put in holes.
- ☐ d. thrown.

———

Add your scores for questions 1–6. Enter the total here and on the graph on page 239.

Total Score ☐

82

Timber for the Indians

In the era before the arrival of the white settlers, the American Indian managed to survive and prosper without any of the inventions of the more advanced European societies. In fact, some of their accomplishments almost defy explanation. The Indians depended heavily on timber for their existence, but how was it that they could cut down trees without the aid of iron axes, indeed, without any metal tools at all?

The Indians solved that problem as they did other problems that confronted them in their wilderness environment—by using good old-fashioned American ingenuity. The hardest material available to the Indian was stone, while the most powerful force they possessed was fire. By combining these two tools, they were able to <u>fell</u> trees quite efficiently.

The Indians made stone hatchets. These were sharpened in preparation for each timber harvest. For a harvest, the Indians first selected the trees to be felled. Then they would build a fire to encircle the bottom of a tree. The flames would burn the trunk in a narrow circular ring near the bottom of the tree. The charred wood could be easily hacked away with a stone axe. When the first charred layer had been cut away, another layer was charred and hacked away, and this procedure was repeated until the tree toppled.

Stone and fire proved to be adequate substitutes for metals, which the Indians never knew existed until the coming of the white settlers.

Main Idea	1		Answer	Score
	Mark the *main idea* ⟶		M	15
	Mark the statement that is *too broad* ⟶		B	5
	Mark the statement that is *too narrow* ⟶		N	5

a. The Indians relied on trees for their existence. ☐ _____

b. Fire was used to fell trees. ☐ _____

c. The Indians used great ingenuity to cut down trees. ☐ _____

**Subject
Matter**

2 The focus of this passage is
- ☐ a. how the Indians built fires.
- ☐ b. how the Indians discovered iron.
- ☐ c. how the Indians felled trees.
- ☐ d. Indians and their customs.   _____

**Supporting
Details**

3 Felling trees was accomplished mainly with the aid of
- ☐ a. fire and vines used as rope.
- ☐ b. stone and fire.
- ☐ c. nature.
- ☐ d. patience.   _____

Conclusion

4 For the Indians, felling trees was a
- ☐ a. job.
- ☐ b. hobby.
- ☐ c. sport.
- ☐ d. custom.   _____

**Clarifying
Devices**

5 The author reveals the Indians' ingenuity with
- ☐ a. a short story.
- ☐ b. a humorous anecdote.
- ☐ c. a documented incident.
- ☐ d. a description of a process.   _____

**Vocabulary
in Context**

6 In this passage the word <u>fell</u> means
- ☐ a. cruel.
- ☐ b. tripped.
- ☐ c. to cut down.
- ☐ d. the hide of an animal.   _____

**Add your scores for questions 1-6. Enter the
total here and on the graph on page 239.**   **Total
Score** ☐

83

Hello!

"Hello" became popular as a greeting with the invention of the telephone. It is said that Alexander Graham Bell, the inventor of the telephone, was the first person to use "hello" in a telephone conversation. For the first several years that telephones were in service, the opening phrase in a conversation was usually, "Are you there?" Perhaps this was because it was difficult for the two parties to hear each other, and because the phones weren't completely reliable. "Hello" quickly became the standard greeting and also started appearing in everyday speech.

Many different words have been used over time to attract a distant person's attention. "Hello" has had many variations throughout the history of the English language. It may have originated as a variation of the familiar "ahoy" that sailors use to hail ships. One early form is probably "hallow," sometimes called the "sailor's hail." In the sixteenth century, a common form was "halloo," or "hallo." Later, there were many variations, such as "hillo," "hilloa," "holla," "holloa," "hullo" and "hollo." Hunters often used these words because their sounds travel well when they are shouted. The Vikings also had a war cry that was similar in sound to these words of greeting. Most calling words and greetings had an <u>echoic</u> origin, because they were meant to travel long distances across water or hills.

Main Idea	1			Answer	Score
		Mark the *main idea*	→	M	15
		Mark the statement that is *too broad*	→	B	5
		Mark the statement that is *too narrow*	→	N	5

a. The greeting "hello" is a fairly new word and has its roots in many other words. ☐ _____

b. "Hello" was popularized by the telephone. ☐ _____

c. There are many ways to greet people. ☐ _____

Score 15 points for each correct answer.   Score

Subject Matter **2** This passage is about

☐ a. mumbling on the telephone.

☐ b. ways of greeting people.

☐ c. shouting messages.

☐ d. spelling errors.   _____

Supporting Details **3** When sailors greet another ship they yell

☐ a. "Hi!"

☐ b. "Hello!"

☐ c. "Ahoy!"

☐ d. "Hallow!"   _____

Conclusion **4** We can infer from this passage that

☐ a. Vikings had very loud voices.

☐ b. the telephone has caused many changes.

☐ c. some words in common use today were derived from similar words used long ago.

☐ d. Alexander Graham Bell was a great man.   _____

Clarifying Devices **5** The writer examines the word *hello* by

☐ a. breaking it down into its Latin and Greek roots.

☐ b. tracing its historic uses as a greeting.

☐ c. comparing it with foreign language greetings.

☐ d. repeating it over and over again.   _____

Vocabulary in Context **6** Echoic means

☐ a. sounding like an echo.

☐ b. hollow.

☐ c. empty.

☐ d. sickly.   _____

Add your scores for questions 1-6. Enter the total here and on the graph on page 239.   Total Score ☐

84

A Mysterious Island

If mysteries fascinate you, you might try looking into the one surrounding Easter Island, which lies in the South Pacific. Ever since the Dutch explorer Jakob Roggeveen discovered the small, isolated island in 1722, experts have remained <u>perplexed</u> as to the origin of the strange artifacts found there.

Roggeveen found the extinct volcanoes on the island interesting, but he was most astonished by the more than 600 huge statues on the island. The statues were almost identical, each carved in the shape of a human head approximately forty feet high and weighing about fifty tons. All the heads gazed sternly out to sea. The figures were carved from a type of volcanic rock called tufa.

Roggeveen later found the quarry where the tufa was mined. He also discovered 150 more partially finished statues, and evidence which seemed to suggest that their sculptors had, for some unknown reason, stopped working rather suddenly.

Many questions remain concerning the strange stone heads of Easter Island. Archaeologists who have investigated the site have uncovered more questions than answers. Many of the statues were discovered to have bodies buried deep in the ground. The reason for this is unknown. Archaeologists have also puzzled over how the enormous stone figures were moved up to ten miles from their original construction sites—a seemingly impossible task, because the island has few trees that could be used as rollers. Further investigations may someday yield the answers to the mysterious questions surrounding Easter Island. But it is just as possible that the mystery will remain forever unsolved.

Main Idea	1		Answer	Score
	Mark the *main idea* ⟶		M	15
	Mark the statement that is *too broad* ⟶		B	5
	Mark the statement that is *too narrow* ⟶		N	5

a. Easter Island contains many mysteries. ☐ _____

b. Easter Island contains huge stone figures whose origins have remained a mystery. ☐ _____

c. Easter Island contains many stone statues. ☐ _____

Subject Matter   **2**   Another good title for this passage might be

- ☐ a. The Life of Dutch Explorer Jakob Roggeveen.
- ☐ b. Statues of Easter Island.
- ☐ c. Archaeological Expeditions in the South Pacific.
- ☐ d. Island of the Aliens.   _____

Supporting Details   **3**   The statues were carved from

- ☐ a. limestone.
- ☐ b. marble.
- ☐ c. granite.
- ☐ d. tufa.   _____

Conclusion   **4**   The origin of the statues of Easter Island

- ☐ a. is known to be alien.
- ☐ b. can be explained by archaeologists.
- ☐ c. is not worth worrying about.
- ☐ d. is still a mystery.   _____

Clarifying Devices   **5**   This story is presented

- ☐ a. in reverse order of events.
- ☐ b. as a logical argument.
- ☐ c. through questions and answers.
- ☐ d. in time sequence.   _____

Vocabulary in Context   **6**   To be <u>perplexed</u> is to be

- ☐ a. confused.
- ☐ b. self-assured.
- ☐ c. doubtful.
- ☐ d. concerned.   _____

Add your scores for questions 1–6. Enter the total here and on the graph on page 239.

Total Score ☐

85

The Great Magician

Harry Houdini was the greatest stunt man and escape artist of all time. No lock, no chain, no manacle could hold him. Locksmiths from all over the world would place supposedly foolproof locks before him, and Houdini would open every one of them. Wherever he went people tested him. The strongest jails in London, Amsterdam, Moscow and the Hague could not hold him. Jailors were embarrassed and truly dumbfounded. "How does he do it?" the world wondered.

Houdini's performances were so fascinating and uncanny that many people believed he possessed supernatural powers. Though he firmly denied using magic, many remained unconvinced.

One of Houdini's favorite stunts was to allow himself to be placed in a straightjacket and bound with iron shackles and chains. His legs were tied together with a sturdy rope and his body was raised. Before an amazed audience, he would wriggle free of his bonds.

It was not until after his death that Houdini's notebooks revealed many of the methods he used to perform the seemingly impossible. Besides being an excellent locksmith, Houdini was a well-conditioned athlete who had superior body control. He was able to contract, stretch or relax virtually any one of his powerful muscles, enabling him to maneuver his way out of the tight fetters designed to hold him.

Main Idea 1

	Answer	Score
Mark the *main idea* ⟶	**M**	15
Mark the statement that is *too broad* ⟶	**B**	5
Mark the statement that is *too narrow* ⟶	**N**	5

a. Houdini was the most skillful and amazing escape artist of all time. ☐ ____

b. Houdini was an amazing man. ☐ ____

c. Houdini was a well-conditioned athlete. ☐ ____

Score 15 points for each correct answer.

Score

Subject Matter

2 This passage is mainly about Houdini's

☐ a. tour of Europe.
☐ b. favorite stunts.
☐ c. muscular contractions.
☐ d. skill as an escape artist.

———

Supporting Details

3 The writer says that Houdini was a

☐ a. jailor.
☐ b. magician.
☐ c. criminal.
☐ d. fine locksmith.

———

Conclusion

4 One can infer from this passage that Houdini's many skills

☐ a. were very easy to learn.
☐ b. did not involve magic.
☐ c. were learned in jail.
☐ d. were learned from great athletes.

———

Clarifying Devices

5 The writer describes Houdini's artistry by using

☐ a. contrasting examples.
☐ b. simple reasoning.
☐ c. various examples.
☐ d. tricks we all know.

———

Vocabulary in Context

6 <u>Bound</u>, in this case, means

☐ a. under obligation.
☐ b. to move by leaps.
☐ c. tied up.
☐ d. on the way to.

———

Add your scores for questions 1-6. Enter the total here and on the graph on page 239.

Total Score ☐

86

His Final Escape

Many accounts have circulated concerning the death of this renowned magician and escape artist. The true story is an interesting but tragic one.

Houdini suffered an ankle injury in October of 1926. On the twenty-second day of that fateful month, he was relaxing in his dressing room at the Princess Theatre in Montreal, the injured foot stretched out before him, when he was visited by a young student from McGill University. The student had previously done a sketch of Houdini, and, having been invited to meet him again, decided to bring two of his friends along. One of them, an amateur boxer named Joselyn Gordon Whitehead, asked Houdini whether he could truly withstand any punch to the belly without flinching, as he had once <u>asserted</u>. Houdini apparently nodded somewhat absent-mindedly, not expecting what followed. Whitehead leaned down and struck him in the abdomen with great force. It is uncertain how many blows were delivered. Houdini gasped and explained that it was necessary to tighten the abdominal muscles before being struck.

Houdini didn't notice any immediate problem after this incident, but during his performance on the following Saturday he felt feverish and weak. He broke down on stage the next Monday, and was immediately given a medical examination. It was discovered that he had suffered a ruptured appendix. Worse, peritonitis, an inflammation of the intestine, had set in. At that time the disease was always fatal, since drugs to combat it had not yet been developed. Although he fought the inevitable, in typical Houdini fashion, for about a week, he finally died on October 31, 1926. He was buried in the family plot in a cemetery in Queens, New York.

Main Idea	1		Answer	Score
	Mark the *main idea* ⟶		M	15
	Mark the statement that is *too broad* ⟶		B	5
	Mark the statement that is *too narrow* ⟶		N	5
	a. Harry Houdini's death was caused by the actions of a careless student.		☐	
	b. It is dangerous to act rashly.		☐	
	c. Harry Houdini contracted peritonitis and died.		☐	

Score 15 points for each correct answer. **Score**

Subject Matter

2 This passage deals mainly with
- [ ] a. the quality of medicine in the 1920s.
- [ ] b. Houdini's final days.
- [ ] c. the death of a famous magician.
- [ ] d. a student's carelessness.

_____

Supporting Details

3 The McGill University student visited Houdini a second time because he
- [ ] a. wanted an autograph.
- [ ] b. wanted to bring a friend.
- [ ] c. wanted to make a sketch.
- [ ] d. had been invited.

_____

Conclusion

4 Harry Houdini died of
- [ ] a. a complication from a broken ankle.
- [ ] b. a ruptured appendix.
- [ ] c. peritonitis, an inflammation of the intestine.
- [ ] d. a breakdown during a performance.

_____

Clarifying Devices

5 The purpose of the first paragraph is to
- [ ] a. provide interesting information as a lead-in.
- [ ] b. make a point about the frequency of rumors concerning celebrities.
- [ ] c. provide details necessary to understanding the story.
- [ ] d. make the account more interesting.

_____

Vocabulary in Context

6 <u>Asserted</u> means
- [ ] a. claimed.
- [ ] b. questioned.
- [ ] c. demanded.
- [ ] d. suggested.

_____

Add your scores for questions 1-6. Enter the total here and on the graph on page 239.

Total Score [ ]

87

A 1,750,000-Year-Old Relative

With his sloping forehead and massive jaw, "Zinj" would today be considered rather unattractive, if not downright ugly. But to archaeologists Mary and Louis Leakey, he is beautiful. Zinj is short for Zinjanthropus, or East African Man, and his remains, dug up by the Leakeys in 1959, proved that primitive people lived on earth over 1,750,000 years ago.

Zinj's remains weren't the only thing the Leakeys found at their digging site in Olduvai Gorge, Tanzania; they also discovered important evidence that revealed the nature of Zinj's prehistoric surroundings and companions. Numerous fossils provided a picture of the extraordinary creatures, now extinct, which competed with Zinj for food. The Leakeys uncovered remains of more than 100 prehistoric giants, among them a pig the size of a hippopotamus and an ostrich two stories tall. These creatures plundered the surrounding vegetation, posing a significant threat to Zinj's survival by limiting his diet to berries, roots and whatever small creatures he could catch with his bare hands. In order to gain access to a richer source of food, he was forced to use the faculty which set him apart from the creatures around him—his ability to think and reason.

Zinj's need for food probably accounts for the crude tools found with him at Olduvai. Zinj had blunt teeth that were ill suited for tearing through the hides of larger animals. But it is believed that by banging and scraping stones together, he produced tools sharp enough to do the job. Zinj's primitive toolmaking was an important step in ensuring the survival of human beings.

Main Idea	1		Answer	Score
		Mark the *main idea* ⟶	M	15
		Mark the statement that is *too broad* ⟶	B	5
		Mark the statement that is *too narrow* ⟶	N	5

a. Prehistoric people were able to survive in their hostile environment by using their ability to think and reason. ☐ ____

b. Prehistoric people lived in a very different environment from the one we live in today. ☐ ____

c. Prehistoric people competed for food with larger animals. ☐

Score 15 points for each correct answer. Score

Subject Matter **2** The best alternate title for this passage would be

☐ a. Mary and Louis Leakey—Archaeologists.

☐ b. Prehistoric People.

☐ c. Zinj's Tools for Survival.

☐ d. East Africa—Birthplace of Humanity. _____

Supporting Details **3** According to the passage, the giant creatures that lived on earth threatened Zinj's survival because

☐ a. he had no weapons to fight them.

☐ b. they destroyed vegetation, a source of food.

☐ c. they preyed upon the small creatures that were Zinj's food sources.

☐ d. they used up the water in the area. _____

Conclusion **4** The statement "But to Mary and Louis Leakey, he is beautiful" implies that

☐ a. the Leakeys have an unusual sense of what is beautiful.

☐ b. Zinj is more attractive than most prehistoric people.

☐ c. the Leakeys felt that what Zinj proved and had to teach about early human life was important.

☐ d. no one else felt the same way. _____

Clarifying Devices **5** In discussing the theory of how Zinj discovered how to make tools, the writer depends mainly on

☐ a. analogies.

☐ b. accounts of actual incidents.

☐ c. statements by archaeologists.

☐ d. reasoning. _____

Vocabulary in Context **6** As used in the passage, <u>faculty</u> means

☐ a. staff.

☐ b. strategy.

☐ c. power of mind.

☐ d. mark. _____

Add your scores for questions 1-6. Enter the total here and on the graph on page 239. Total Score ☐

88

Blowing Their Tops

The eruption of Mount St. Helens, in the state of Washington, is only the latest in a long line of spectacular volcanic eruptions that have occurred over the past hundred years. Let's look at previous eruptions. In 1902, Mount Pelee in Martinique exploded, shooting out a huge cloud of burning gas and ashes that killed the 30,000 citizens of St. Pierre. An 1883 eruption, which blew the top off the island of Krakatoa, near Sumatra, created a tidal wave that killed 36,000 people. When Mount Bezumyannaya erupted in Siberia in 1956, it spit out 2.4 billion tons of rock—enough debris to bury the city of Paris. Although its ashes were carried over 250 miles, no one was killed, because the volcano was in a <u>remote</u> area.

In February of 1943, near the Mexican village of Paricutin, a man watched a volcano emerge in his cornfield. Dionisio Pulido was work- ing in his field when a small crack in the ground began to expand and the earth started to shake. The stunned farmer watched until the danger forced him to leave. Out of the rift poured a cloud of smoke and sparks so large that at night it created a fireworks display that was visible for over fifty miles. By late March, the cloud had grown to a 20,000-foot column of smoke that was raining ashes on Mexico City, 200 miles away. Before the newborn volcano finally subsided, in 1952, it had created a mountain 1,200 feet high, where Pulido's cornfield had been.

Main Idea 1

	Answer	Score
Mark the *main idea* ⟶	M	15
Mark the statement that is *too broad* ⟶	B	5
Mark the statement that is *too narrow* ⟶	N	5

a. Many volcanoes have erupted over the past hundred years. ☐ _____

b. In Mexico, a volcano sprang up in a farmer's cornfield. ☐ _____

c. Erupting volcanoes can be very destructive. ☐ _____

Subject Matter

2 The passage is <u>primarily</u> about

☐ a. great disasters.
☐ b. volcanic eruptions.
☐ c. Mount St. Helens.
☐ d. a volcano in Mexico. _____

Supporting Details

3 According to the passage, Mount Bezumyannaya in Siberia

☐ a. emerged in a cornfield.
☐ b. caused a tidal wave.
☐ c. killed 36,000 people.
☐ d. killed no one. _____

Conclusion

4 We can conclude from the passage that volcanoes

☐ a. do not occur anymore.
☐ b. occur in many different parts of the world.
☐ c. are really not terribly dangerous.
☐ d. usually erupt in the winter. _____

Clarifying Devices

5 The story of the volcano in the cornfield is presented to demonstrate the fact that volcanoes

☐ a. kill a lot of people.
☐ b. erupt in Mexico.
☐ c. spring up from level ground.
☐ d. have often been unpredictable. _____

Vocabulary in Context

6 In this passage <u>remote</u> is closest in meaning to

☐ a. isolated.
☐ b. lonely.
☐ c. rural.
☐ d. barren. _____

Add your scores for questions 1-6. Enter the total here and on the graph on page 239.

Total Score ☐

89

The Master Forger

The literary giants of the past have always been prey to clever forgers desiring wealth and borrowed fame. One of the more popular targets of forgers has been William Shakespeare. Probably the most successful of all Shakespeare forgers was an eighteen-year-old boy named William Henry Ireland.

Ireland, the son of a respected book dealer, perpetrated his hoax on the literary public in the late eighteenth century. The boy's success rested on his astonishing skill both in imitating Shakespeare's style and in producing documents with an appearance of age and authenticity.

Ireland claimed that the works he forged were written by Shakespeare. He based his claim on a deed, supposedly signed by Shakespeare, in which the Bard <u>bequeathed</u> certain of his books and papers to a William Henry Ireland, whom young Ireland claimed as an ancestor. His inheritance, the boy revealed, consisted of letters by Shakespeare to his wife, two plays, and legal contracts and receipts signed by the playwright. Outstanding scholars, critics and poets examined the "finds," and, except for Edmund Malone, the leading Shakespearean expert of the day, all proclaimed them authentic. Richard Sheridan bought the play *Vortigern and Rowena* and produced it with a star cast at his Drury Lane theatre.

The play's presentation helped Malone convince other skeptics of the hoax, and Ireland finally confessed. However, Ireland had the last laugh. The controversy created a market for his phony Shakespearean works, and Ireland seized the opportunity and did a brisk and profitable business making and selling imitations of his imitations.

Main Idea	1		Answer	Score
	Mark the *main idea* ⟶	M		15
	Mark the statement that is *too broad* ⟶	B		5
	Mark the statement that is *too narrow* ⟶	N		5

a. Ireland was a highly successful forger of Shakespearean works and documents. ☐ ____

b. There have been many attempted forgeries of William Shakespeare's works. ☐ ____

c. *Vortigern and Rowena* was a play forged by W.H. Ireland. ☐ ____

Score 15 points for each correct answer.   **Score**

Subject Matter **2** The passage is primarily about
- [ ] a. William Shakespeare.
- [ ] b. literary forgery.
- [ ] c. the forged play *Vortigern and Rowena*.
- [ ] d. William Henry Ireland's hoax.   _____

Supporting Details **3** How did Ireland claim to have received the Shakespearean documents?
- [ ] a. He said he bought them from Richard Sheridan.
- [ ] b. He said they were deeded to an ancestor and he inherited them.
- [ ] c. He said they were given to him by Edmund Malone.
- [ ] d. He said his father, a book dealer, bought them at an auction.   _____

Conclusion **4** We can conclude that Ireland
- [ ] a. did not forge the Shakespearean documents.
- [ ] b. helped his father forge the documents.
- [ ] c. was successful because he was bold.
- [ ] d. had no talent as a playwright or a poet.   _____

Clarifying Devices **5** "However, Ireland had the last laugh" means
- [ ] a. most critics still believed Ireland.
- [ ] b. Ireland thought his hoax was funny.
- [ ] c. Ireland had a better sense of humor than his critics.
- [ ] d. Ireland made money from his hoax even after it was discovered.   _____

Vocabulary in Context **6** As used in the passage, the word <u>bequeathed</u> means
- [ ] a. sold.
- [ ] b. sent.
- [ ] c. gave.
- [ ] d. offered.   _____

Add your scores for questions 1–6. Enter the total here and on the graph on page 239.   **Total Score** [   ]

90

Don't Fool Around with Camels!

Most people think of a camel as an obedient beast of burden, because it is best known for its ability to carry heavy loads across vast stretches of desert without requiring water. In reality, the camel is considerably more than just the Arabian equivalent of the mule. It also possesses a great amount of intelligence and sensitivity.

The Arabs assert that camels are so acutely aware of injustice and ill treatment that a camel owner who punishes one of the beasts too harshly finds it difficult to escape the camel's vengeance. Apparently, the animal will remember an injury and wait for an opportunity to get revenge.

In order to protect themselves from the vengeful beasts, Arabian camel drivers have learned to trick their camels into believing they have achieved revenge. When an Arab realizes that he has excited a camel's rage, he places his own garments on the ground in the animal's path. He arranges the clothing so that it appears to cover a man's body. When the camel recognizes its master's clothing on the ground, it seizes the pile with its teeth, shakes the garments violently and tramples on them in a frenzy. Eventually, after its anger has subsided, the camel departs, assuming its revenge is complete. Only then does the owner of the garments come out of hiding, safe for the time being, thanks to this clever <u>ruse.</u>

Main Idea   1

	Answer	Score
Mark the *main idea* ⟶	M	15
Mark the statement that is *too broad* ⟶	B	5
Mark the statement that is *too narrow* ⟶	N	5

a. Camels are sensitive to injustice and will seek revenge on those who harm them. ☐ _____

b. Camel drivers are often the targets of camels' revenge. ☐ _____

c. Camels are sensitive creatures that are aware of injustice. ☐ _____

Subject Matter

2 The best alternate title for this passage would be

- ☐ a. The Life of a Camel Driver.
- ☐ b. The Camel's Revenge.
- ☐ c. In the Desert.
- ☐ d. The Fearsome Camel. _____

Supporting Details

3 According to the passage, camels

- ☐ a. never drink water.
- ☐ b. are always violent.
- ☐ c. are very sensitive.
- ☐ d. are rarely used anymore. _____

Conclusion

4 From this passage we can conclude that

- ☐ a. camels are generally vicious toward their owners.
- ☐ b. camels are easily deceived.
- ☐ c. camels don't see very well.
- ☐ d. camels try to punish people who abuse them. _____

Clarifying Devices

5 The writer makes the camel's vengeful behavior clearer to the reader by presenting

- ☐ a. a well-planned argument.
- ☐ b. a large variety of examples.
- ☐ c. some eyewitness accounts.
- ☐ d. a typical incident. _____

Vocabulary in Context

6 The best definition for the word <u>ruse</u> is

- ☐ a. a deception or hoax.
- ☐ b. a joke.
- ☐ c. a game.
- ☐ d. a beast of burden. _____

Add your scores for questions 1-6. Enter the total here and on the graph on page 239.

Total Score ☐

91

Forced to Try Anything

The instinct for self-preservation is a strong one and can inspire some unusual behavior. During the fourteenth century, when the infamous plague, the Black Death, raged through Europe, fear of contamination was a strong force that motivated people to try strange things in order to save themselves.

In Lubeck, Germany, the panicked citizens believed the plague was a manifestation of the wrath of God. They tried to appease this anger by bringing money and riches to the churches. At one church, the monks, fearing contaminations themselves, would not let the people enter. So the crowd threw their gold and jewels over the walls only to have them tossed back by the cautious priests. The valuables were finally allowed to pile up, and they remained untouched for months.

During this epidemic, people tried every imaginable plague preventative and remedy. Many people believed that sitting between two great fires might be a preventative. There was an attempt to wipe out the swallow population, because it was widely believed that swallows transmitted the disease. Allowing birds to fly about the sickroom was also tried, on the theory that the birds would absorb the airborne poisons.

All varieties of unpleasant substances were used, in the belief that they would help to prevent or cure the plague. These attempts ranged from smoking tobacco to placing dried toads or the insides of pigeons or newborn puppies over the boils caused by the disease. Interestingly, smoking may actually have had some positive effect. Smoke drove away the plague-bearing flies.

Main Idea	1		Answer	Score
		Mark the *main idea* ⟶	M	15
		Mark the statement that is *too broad* ⟶	B	5
		Mark the statement that is *too narrow* ⟶	N	5
		a. The instinct for survival is very strong.	☐	____
		b. The desire to avoid the plague caused some unusual behavior.	☐	____
		c. Smoking may have helped to save some people from the plague.	☐	____

Score 15 points for each correct answer. **Score**

Subject Matter

2 The best alternate title for this passage would be

☐ a. Smoking and the Plague.

☐ b. Causes of the Black Plague.

☐ c. An Incident at Lubeck.

☐ d. The Fear of Contamination. _____

Supporting Details

3 During the plague, some people brought birds into the sickroom because they believed they

☐ a. were a sign of good luck.

☐ b. carried the plague.

☐ c. carried antibodies for the disease.

☐ d. absorbed poisons in the air. _____

Conclusion

4 The second paragraph implies that

☐ a. the instinct for survival is stronger than greed.

☐ b. rich and powerful persons have special immunity to disease.

☐ c. people are overly cautious about contagious diseases.

☐ d. the wrath of God brought on the plague. _____

Clarifying Devices

5 The main idea of this passage is developed mainly through the use of

☐ a. deductive reasoning.

☐ b. examples.

☐ c. comparisons.

☐ d. logical arguments. _____

Vocabulary in Context

6 A <u>manifestation</u> is

☐ a. an example.

☐ b. a result.

☐ c. a display.

☐ d. an indication. _____

Add your scores for questions 1-6. Enter the total here and on the graph on page 239.

Total Score ☐

92

Dodgson's Dictionary

Dictionaries are not closed books. There is still plenty of room for more words in these voluminous vocabulary authorities. New words are continually being created and added to our language. And most of today's wordsmiths can credit a famous mathematician with the creation of the method by which they develop many new words. The mathematician was an Englishman named Charles L. Dodgson. In addition to working with figures, Dodgson wrote books. His imaginative stories and poems have made Dodgson beloved to generations of readers. We know him, however, not by the name of Dodgson, but by his pseudonym, Lewis Carroll.

Lewis Carroll has delighted countless readers, young and old, with *Alice in Wonderland, Through the Looking Glass* and numerous poems. In these works, Carroll developed dozens of nonsensical words such as "chortle" and "galumph." Many of these words eventually blended imperceptibly with other more conventional words of the English language. Carroll referred to his made-up words as "portmanteau" words, named after a kind of leather suitcase that opens into two compartments. The name was well suited, because most of Carroll's words had two compartments. Rather than being entirely fabricated, they were usually made from the combined parts of two different words. A "snark," for example, clearly came from a snake and a shark. Although Carroll died long ago, his technique continues to be used today. We can clearly see his influence in words such as *smog, brunch,* and *guesstimation.*

Main Idea	1		Answer	Score
	Mark the *main idea* ⟶		M	15
	Mark the statement that is *too broad* ⟶		B	5
	Mark the statement that is *too narrow* ⟶		N	5

a. Dodgson, better known as Lewis Carroll, developed a method for making new words by combining parts of two existing words. ☐ _____

b. Charles Dodgson contributed to the English language. ☐ _____

c. Dodgson made up words in the stories and poems he wrote. ☐ _____

Score 15 points for each correct answer.   **Score**

Subject Matter

2 This passage is about

☐ a. the story *Alice in Wonderland*.
☐ b. mathematics.
☐ c. how a dictionary is written.
☐ d. how Charles Dodgson created new words. _____

Supporting Details

3 Dodgson's made-up words

☐ a. are borrowed from "real" words.
☐ b. are totally ridiculous.
☐ c. come from Greek.
☐ d. always begin with *s*.   _____

Conclusion

4 We can conclude from this passage that Dodgson was

☐ a. better known for his writing than for his work in mathematics.
☐ b. a fine mathematician.
☐ c. perhaps a little crazy.
☐ d. fascinated with dictionaries.   _____

Clarifying Devices

5 The first sentence of this passage uses

☐ a. irony.
☐ b. a play on words.
☐ c. a foreign phrase.
☐ d. one of Dodgson's words.   _____

Vocabulary in Context

6 A pseudonym is

☐ a. a nickname.
☐ b. a false name.
☐ c. a family name.
☐ d. a foreign name.   _____

Add your scores for questions 1–6. Enter the total here and on the graph on page 239.

Total Score ☐

207

93

Hearing Hazards

Pardon me? As you get older, you may notice that your hearing is not as sharp as it once was. Age does affect hearing. However, hearing loss is most likely to occur because of exposure to constant sounds in your daily life.

The American Speech and Hearing Association has estimated that 40 million Americans are subjected every day to dangerously high levels of noise. Sound is measured in decibels, and studies show that permanent hearing <u>impairment</u> can result from exposure to sound levels of about eighty-five decibels. Many high decibel noises come from machines, but machines are not the only producers of painfully loud noises. A screaming baby, at ninety decibels, is more damaging to the sensitive inner ear than a vacuum cleaner at seventy decibels, street traffic at seventy-five decibels, or an alarm clock at eighty. Prolonged exposure to the blare of a jackhammer, whose noise level reaches 100 decibels, a power mower at 105 decibels, an auto horn at 120 decibels, or a jet engine at 140 decibels can cause permanent damage to a person's hearing.

Obviously, people such as airplane pilots or construction workers, who are regularly exposed to loud noises, should take precautions to protect their hearing. A survey done by the New York League for the Hard of Hearing clearly points up one of these occupational hazards. The study indicates that 50 percent of all rock and roll disc jockeys have suffered hearing damage. Of these, 33 percent have become partially deaf.

Main Idea 1

	Answer	Score
Mark the *main idea* ⟶	M	15
Mark the statement that is *too broad* ⟶	B	5
Mark the statement that is *too narrow* ⟶	N	5

a. Noises in our everyday lives may cause hearing damage. ☐ _____

b. Many occupations have hidden dangers. ☐ _____

c. Loud machine noises often cause damage to hearing. ☐ _____

Score 15 points for each correct answer.   **Score**

Subject Matter

2 This passage is mostly about

☐ a. how sound is measured.

☐ b. the effect of loud noises on hearing.

☐ c. the sensitivity of the inner ear.

☐ d. the effect of sound on disc jockeys.   _____

Supporting Details

3 According to the passage, airplane pilots should be concerned about their hearing because

☐ a. most pilots suffer hearing loss.

☐ b. high altitudes put pressure on the ear.

☐ c. the sound of a jet engine can cause permanent hearing damage.

☐ d. noise levels in airport terminals are hazardous.   _____

Conclusion

4 We can conclude from the passage that

☐ a. most jet pilots become deaf.

☐ b. hearing loss is more likely to be caused by old age than by high noise levels.

☐ c. 40 million Americans have suffered permanent damage to their hearing.

☐ d. someone employed as a jackhammer operator may suffer permanent hearing loss.   _____

Clarifying Devices

5 The writer mentions that a study showed that "50 percent of all rock and roll disc jockeys have suffered hearing damage" in order to

☐ a. show that rock and roll may be more harmful than other types of music.

☐ b. disprove claims that rock and roll music has safe decibel levels.

☐ c. show that certain occupations have high levels of noise that can cause hearing loss.

☐ d. get an emotional response from the reader.   _____

Vocabulary in Context

6 The word <u>impairment</u> is closest in meaning to

☐ a. sensitivity.

☐ b. change.

☐ c. improvement.

☐ d. damage.   _____

Add your scores for questions 1–6. Enter the total here and on the graph on page 239.   Total Score ☐

94

Maker of Great Violins

Hundreds of violins are made every day. However, the finest and most sought after violins ever made were handcrafted by an Italian violin maker over two hundred and fifty years ago. The craftsman's name was Antonius Stradivarius. Any one of his violins is worth more than $100,000 today.

Stradivarius was born in 1644. He began his career as a violin maker's apprentice. Working on his own by 1680, he became determined to make instruments that could reproduce tones as <u>rich</u> as those produced by the human voice. He tested several shapes and styles for his violins, until he arrived at a design that pleased him. During his career he crafted over eleven hundred violins. Those still in existence have become treasured possessions.

Unfortunately, the secret of the Stradivarius violin died with its maker. During his lifetime Stradivarius kept his notes safely hidden. Even his two sons, who helped him in his workshop, did not know all the steps involved in each violin's construction.

Through the years, many experts have offered possible explanations for the unique tone of a "Strad." Some say it is the instrument's shape and the harmony of its parts. Others suggest that the secret lies in the special properties of the wood, which Stradivarius obtained from native Italian trees that no longer exist. The most widely accepted supposition is that the exquisite tone of the violins is created by the varnish that the old master used to coat his instruments. Chemists have analyzed and reproduced, as closely as possible, this varnish, and its application has improved the sound of many violins. Still, no violin maker has been able to fully reproduce the tone of Stradivarius's violins.

Main Idea	1		Answer	Score
		Mark the *main idea* ⟶	**M**	15
		Mark the statement that is *too broad* ⟶	**B**	5
		Mark the statement that is *too narrow* ⟶	**N**	5
		a. Stradivarius crafted the world's finest violins.	☐	____
		b. Stradivarius was an Italian violin maker.	☐	____
		c. Stradivarius was an extremely talented craftsman.	☐	____

Subject Matter

2 Another good title for this passage would be

☐ a. How to Make Violins.

☐ b. Expensive Violins.

☐ c. Stradivarius's Secret.

☐ d. Italian Violin Makers.　　　　_____

Supporting Details

3 According to this passage, Stradivarius made

☐ a. hundreds of violins every day.

☐ b. over 100,000 violins during his career.

☐ c. only one violin.

☐ d. hundreds of violins during his career.　　_____

Conclusion

4 We can conclude from the passage that Stradivarius's

☐ a. notes were found by chemists.

☐ b. notes were never found.

☐ c. secrets were learned when he was an apprentice.

☐ d. notes were left to his sons.　　　　_____

Clarifying Devices

5 The writer shows the uniqueness of Stradivarius's violins by stating that

☐ a. Stradivarius made only 1,100 violins.

☐ b. all of Stradivarius's violins were varnished.

☐ c. Stradivarius experimented with different styles.

☐ d. no one has been able to duplicate the sound of Stradivarius's violins.　　_____

Vocabulary in Context

6 In this passage the word <u>rich</u> means

☐ a. wealthy.

☐ b. highly amusing.

☐ c. full and mellow.

☐ d. producing or yielding abundantly.　　_____

Add your scores for questions 1-6. Enter the total here and on the graph on page 239.　　Total Score ☐

211

95

Funeral for a Fly

You've undoubtedly heard that some people have funerals for their pets. These are usually animals that have been true and loyal companions. Still, you might be surprised to hear that the brilliant Roman poet Virgil, who lived from 70 to 19 B.C., had a funeral for his pet fly.

When the second triumvirate came into power in Rome, in 43 B.C., the three leaders—Augustus, Marc Antony and Lepidus—enacted a law which transferred portions of land from the rich to the poorer war veterans. There were only a few exceptions. Among those parcels of land exempted from the decree were cemeteries and mausoleums.

Virgil, on hearing that his own villa might be slated for confiscation as well, devised a plan to save his property. He arranged a funeral and subsequent burial for a fly, pretending it was a much loved pet. The burial took place as part of a lavish ceremony, amid much pomp and circumstance. The ceremony featured speeches by a number of prominent Romans, including Virgil himself, bereaving the loss of the fly. The cost of this elaborate affair came to over $150,000 in today's currency.

As a result of the ruse, after the ceremony, Virgil's house was considered a mausoleum and was exempted from the provisions of the ordinance.

Main Idea	1		Answer	Score
	Mark the *main idea* ⟶		M	15
	Mark the statement that is *too broad* ⟶		B	5
	Mark the statement that is *too narrow* ⟶		N	5

a. Virgil had a funeral for his pet fly. ☐ ____

b. Virgil found a way to avoid losing his property. ☐ ____

c. Virgil devised an elaborate burial ceremony for a fly, to avoid having to comply with an ordinance. ☐ ____

Score 15 points for each correct answer.   **Score**

Subject Matter

2 This passage is about

☐ a. Roman politics in the first century B.C.
☐ b. an expensive legal loophole.
☐ c. Virgil's pet fly.
☐ d. Roman burial customs.   _____

Supporting Details

3 The lands of the rich were to be confiscated in order to

☐ a. give poor farmers more land.
☐ b. increase taxes for the state.
☐ c. provide war veterans with land.
☐ d. divide the land more evenly among the city dwellers.   _____

Conclusion

4 One can conclude from the passage that

☐ a. Virgil didn't really love the fly.
☐ b. Virgil didn't really bury a fly.
☐ c. flies were common pets in Roman households.
☐ d. the graves of pets were not considered exempt from the ordinance.   _____

Clarifying Devices

5 The information in the second paragraph is necessary to the story because it

☐ a. adds interesting historical background.
☐ b. gives relevant information necessary to the story.
☐ c. serves as an expanding element in story development.
☐ d. is a smooth transition from the first to the third paragraph.   _____

Vocabulary in Context

6 Subsequent means

☐ a. contemporary.
☐ b. simultaneous.
☐ c. ensuing.
☐ d. extemporaneous.   _____

Add your scores for questions 1-6. Enter the total here and on the graph on page 239.

Total
Score ☐

96

The Greatly Feared Octopus

The octopus's reputation as a human-killer isn't simply an exaggeration—it is a total myth. The octopus can indeed be a deadly hunter, but only of its natural prey. Clams, mussels, crabs, lobsters and an occasional sick or unwary fish have reason to be frightened of this multi-armed predator, but a person is much too large to interest even the biggest octopus. Even a giant among octopi is much smaller than most people imagine. Far from being large enough to <u>engulf</u> a submarine, as monster octopi in movies have been known to do, the largest octopi, found on the Pacific coast, weigh around 110 pounds and grow to a diameter of no more than ten feet.

The hard, parrotlike beak of an octopus is not used for attacking deep-sea divers, but for cutting open crabs and lobsters. Indeed, the octopus possesses such a tiny throat that it cannot swallow large pieces of meat. It feeds instead by pouring digestive juices into its victims, and then sucking up the soupy remains. A clam or scallop that finds itself in the grasp of an octopus has only a short time to live. But human beings are perfectly safe. Still, people rarely care to venture close enough to these timid creatures to get a good look at them.

Main Idea 1

	Answer	Score
Mark the *main idea* ⟶	M	15
Mark the statement that is *too broad* ⟶	B	5
Mark the statement that is *too narrow* ⟶	N	5

a. The octopus is not dangerous, as many people believe it to be. ☐ ____

b. People often fear creatures that are not dangerous to them. ☐ ____

c. The octopus only hunts its natural prey. ☐ ____

Score 15 points for each correct answer. **Score**

Subject Matter

2 This passage is mainly about
- [ ] a. the horrors of the octopus.
- [ ] b. the largest octopus in the world.
- [ ] c. the octopus's deadly hunting methods.
- [ ] d. octopi and their behavior.   _____

Supporting Details

3 The passage states that octopi
- [ ] a. use their eight tentacles to catch their prey.
- [ ] b. always catch sick and careless fish.
- [ ] c. never attack people.
- [ ] d. can engulf submarines.   _____

Conclusion

4 You would not expect octopi to
- [ ] a. kill clams.
- [ ] b. approach divers underwater.
- [ ] c. hide from danger.
- [ ] d. suck up their prey.   _____

Clarifying Devices

5 The author attempts to dispel people's misplaced fears about octopi by
- [ ] a. contrasting facts with common misconceptions.
- [ ] b. telling lies about the creatures.
- [ ] c. pretending to like octopi.
- [ ] d. making jokes about ocean life.   _____

Vocabulary in Context

6 Engulf means
- [ ] a. surround.
- [ ] b. beach.
- [ ] c. kill.
- [ ] d. out race.   _____

Add your scores for questions 1-6. Enter the total here and on the graph on page 239.   **Total Score** ☐

97

The World's Largest Diamond

In 1907, King Edward VII of England received an <u>extravagant</u> present for his sixty-sixth birthday: a diamond that weighed 3,106 carats.

This raw, rough diamond was found on January 25, 1905, in South Africa. A mine superintendent named Frederick Wells, stumbled across it while inspecting the Premier Mine before closing it down for the day. The diamond, which was named after the founder of the mine, Thomas Cullinan, turned out to be the largest diamond ever discovered. Wells not only picked up a giant jewel that day, but a $10,000 reward as well.

With the King's birthday in mind, the South African government purchased this large uncut stone. When the king finally received his priceless present, it was still in its original form, so he had to have the diamond properly cut and polished. After a lengthy search, Joseph Asscher, a Dutch craftsman, was chosen to perform the delicate operation.

In 1908, after weeks of study and inspection, Joseph Asscher finally concluded that the best plan was to cleave the Cullinan diamond into nine major stones, ninety-six lesser gems, and ten carats of polished fragments.

The most magnificent of the nine major stones cut from the Cullinan is the 530-carat, pear-shaped gem known as the Great Star of Africa. Today this stone is part of the royal scepter of the British crown jewels, which are carefully guarded in the famous Tower of London.

Main Idea	1		Answer	Score
	Mark the *main idea* ⟶	M		15
	Mark the statement that is *too broad* ⟶	B		5
	Mark the statement that is *too narrow* ⟶	N		5
	a. Diamonds are magnificent gems worthy of a king.	☐		____
	b. The Cullinan diamond is part of the crown jewels of England.	☐		____
	c. The Cullinan diamond was the largest and most magnificent diamond ever found.	☐		____

Subject Matter　　**2**　What is the main subject of the passage?

☐ a. King Edward VII
☐ b. Joseph Asscher
☐ c. The Cullinan diamond
☐ d. The British crown jewels　　　　　———

Supporting Details　　**3**　The Cullinan diamond was found in the

☐ a. South African Mine.
☐ b. Premier Mine.
☐ c. Nile Mine.
☐ d. Wells Mine.　　　　　———

Conclusion　　**4**　You can assume from this passage that

☐ a. King Edward VII was fond of diamonds.
☐ b. the Cullinan diamond was hard to find.
☐ c. Frederick Wells liked King Edward VII.
☐ d. Joseph Asscher was skilled at cutting diamonds.　　　　　———

Clarifying Devices　　**5**　In the first sentence, the writer calls attention to the subject by telling about an incredible

☐ a. piece of rock.
☐ b. birthday gift.
☐ c. sparkler.
☐ d. crown jewel.　　　　　———

Vocabulary in Context　　**6**　In this passage extravagant means

☐ a. rare.
☐ b. very impractical.
☐ c. extremely nice.
☐ d. tasteful.　　　　　———

Add your scores for questions 1–6. Enter the total here and on the graph on page 239.　　Total Score ☐

98

Beyond the Call of Duty

The marathon, a regular event in the Olympic Games, got its name from the Greek plain of Marathon, where a battle between the Persian army, led by King Darius, and the Athenian army was fought in 490 B.C.

Darius's troops had arrived on Marathon and were preparing to attack Athens. The Athenians were greatly outnumbered by the Persians, so they sent a runner, Pheidippides, to Sparta to request aid against the attackers. Pheidippides ran the 140 miles to Sparta in about twenty-four hours. After receiving a promise of help from the Spartans, he ran back to deliver the news, again covering the rocky <u>terrain</u> in twenty-four hours.

Pheidippides fought in the battle of Marathon several days later. The Spartans didn't come to their aid in time, but the Athenians were victorious anyway. The commander of the army wanted to notify the citizens of Athens of the Persians' defeat. The battle-weary Pheidippides, who had had little time to recover from his 280-mile run of the previous week, agreed to be the messenger.

He set off on the nearly twenty-five-mile-long trek from Marathon to Athens, and ran into the Athenian marketplace just a few hours later. He gasped "Rejoice, we conquer," then dropped dead in his tracks before the astounded onlookers.

The marathon footrace was established as an Olympic event in honor of Pheidippides. The official distance for a marathon is 26 miles, 385 yards.

Main Idea 1

	Answer	Score
Mark the *main idea* ⟶	M	15
Mark the statement that is *too broad* ⟶	B	5
Mark the statement that is *too narrow* ⟶	N	5

a. Pheidippides was a Greek hero in whose honor the marathon footrace was instituted. ☐ ____

b. Pheidippides is a hero of Greek history. ☐ ____

c. Pheidippides ran as a messenger for the Athenian army. ☐ ____

Score 15 points for each correct answer.   **Score**

2 This passage deals mainly with

☐ a. a battle between the Greeks and the
Romans.

☐ b. the origin of the Olympic event called
the marathon.

☐ c. a Greek runner's heroic endurance.

☐ d. the Athenian army's victory against the
Persian army.   _____

3 Pheidippides first ran to

☐ a. request supplies from neighbors.

☐ b. announce that the Persians were going to
attack Sparta.

☐ c. request aid from allies.

☐ d. demand reasons for the attack.   _____

4 We can conclude from this passage that

☐ a. Pheidippides loved his country.

☐ b. the Athenian commander was merciless.

☐ c. the Spartans didn't want to help the
Athenians.

☐ d. marathon races are not difficult to run. _____

5 The words "battle-weary Pheidippides" are
meant to make the reader feel

☐ a. angry toward the Persians.

☐ b. interested in the battle.

☐ c. bored with the outcome of the battle.

☐ d. sympathetic toward Pheidippides.   _____

6 Terrain means

☐ a. hills.

☐ b. paths.

☐ c. plain.

☐ d. land.   _____

**Add your scores for questions 1-6. Enter the
total here and on the graph on page 239.**

**Total
Score**

99

Victorious Crickets

Crickets, in the ordinary scheme of things, are unexceptional insects. But in ancient China, crickets were the heroes of a national pastime. They were highly trained athletes.

People would search the fields rigorously for the biggest and strongest crickets that could be found. Then these carefully selected crickets were cared for according to a regular routine. They were always well fed, to keep them strong and heavy, and they were prodded into exercising by being forced to jump and jump until they were exhausted. In this manner, the crickets' muscles were built up to far beyond ordinary cricket strength. When the owner-trainer felt his cricket was in tip-top shape, he would announce a challenge. A public bout would take place.

Like the gladiators of Rome, crickets were forced to face each other in high-stake duels to the death. They were placed in a small pit, and a referee irritated their sensitive antennae, to goad them into attacking one another. The insects would scuttle toward one another and attempt to rip each other apart. The survivor, of course, was a much celebrated and applauded insect, especially if several bets had been placed on it and the cricket had earned some members of the audience a few dollars. Extremely successful crickets could be sold for $100 each, and there was a rumor that one cricket made over $90,000 in winnings for its owner. When this champion of champions died, it was <u>interred</u> in a miniature silver coffin and given the honorable title "Victorious Cricket."

Main Idea 1

	Answer	Score
Mark the *main idea* ⟶	M	15
Mark the statement that is *too broad* ⟶	B	5
Mark the statement that is *too narrow* ⟶	N	5

a. In ancient China, cricket dueling was a form of amusement and a basis for betting. ☐ ____

b. Successful crickets were sold for high prices. ☐ ____

c. In ancient China, crickets provided a popular form of entertainment. ☐ ____

Subject Matter

2 The topic of this passage is

- ☐ a. famous pet crickets.
- ☐ b. dueling crickets.
- ☐ c. Chinese customs.
- ☐ d. a dead champion.   _____

Supporting Details

3 "Victorious Cricket" was buried in a

- ☐ a. pet cemetery.
- ☐ b. country cemetery.
- ☐ c. tiny silver coffin.
- ☐ d. small grave.   _____

Conclusion

4 In the third paragraph, the author implies that crickets were

- ☐ a. armed with sharp spurs.
- ☐ b. not willing to fight of their own accord.
- ☐ c. not very vicious fighters.
- ☐ d. rewarded with a good meal.   _____

Clarifying Devices

5 The phrase "of course" in the third paragraph identifies an

- ☐ a. easily answered question.
- ☐ b. argument.
- ☐ c. obvious statement.
- ☐ d. expected comparison.   _____

Vocabulary in Context

6 The word <u>interred</u> means

- ☐ a. pasted on.
- ☐ b. buried in a graveyard.
- ☐ c. set adrift on a stream.
- ☐ d. encased in concrete.   _____

Add your scores for questions 1-6. Enter the total here and on the graph on page 239.   **Total Score** ☐

100

A Short Career

With his expressive style and subtly mysterious imagery, Jean Nicholas Arthur Rimbaud, the nineteenth century Frenchman known as the father of the Symbolist movement, had an unquestionably profound effect on modern poetry. The older poet Verlaine, greatly influenced by Rimbaud, drew critical attention to him. This helped place the young man at the head of the new literary movement that was stirring in France.

But Rimbaud seems to have had little desire to lead the way. In fact, his life as a poet lasted only from the time he was fifteen until he was twenty. He spent his early twenties wandering through Europe in drunken debauchery, often ill or acutely poverty-stricken, and apparently writing nothing to fulfill the brilliant promise of his teens. He finally renounced his art completely. Rimbaud traveled to North Africa and became manager of a trading station, exporting coffee, gum, and ivory, and engaging in the profitable traffic of arms and ammunition.

Scholars are certain that Rimbaud was aware of his growing renown in Europe, which resulted from the publication, in his absence, of his poetic collection *Illuminations*. Enthusiasts in France wrote to him, requesting his return to head the Symbolist movement. He chose to stay in Ethiopia.

Rimbaud died at the age of thirty-seven, having written nothing since his twentieth birthday. His poetry continues to be the <u>focus</u> of critical attention and admiration, and is still a model for poets, despite the fact that it was written by a teenage boy.

		Answer	Score
Main Idea 1			
	Mark the *main idea* ———————→	**M**	15
	Mark the statement that is *too broad* ———→	**B**	5
	Mark the statement that is *too narrow* ———→	**N**	5
	a. Rimbaud gave up poetry for business.	☐	___
	b. Young poets such as Rimbaud have influenced generations of poets.	☐	___
	c. Rimbaud wrote brilliant and lasting poetry as a teenager, but ultimately rejected his art and fame.	☐	___

Score 15 points for each correct answer.   **Score**

Subject Matter

2 This passage is mostly about Rimbaud's

- ☐ a. influence on the Symbolist poets.
- ☐ b. poetic style.
- ☐ c. life and career.
- ☐ d. debt to Verlaine.

_____

Supporting Details

3 According to the passage, while he was in North Africa, Rimbaud's fame grew in Europe because

- ☐ a. a collection of his poems was published.
- ☐ b. Verlaine told critics about him.
- ☐ c. he sent his poetry to enthusiasts in France.
- ☐ d. the Symbolists were using his poetry as a model.

_____

Conclusion

4 The last paragraph of the passage implies that

- ☐ a. Rimbaud's poetry is noteworthy because it was written by a teenager.
- ☐ b. Rimbaud's poetry is less critically acclaimed than it was in his lifetime.
- ☐ c. it is surprising that a teenager's work was good enough to have had such lasting value and influence.
- ☐ d. Rimbaud's work does not deserve the attention and admiration it receives.

_____

Clarifying Devices

5 The writer develops the story by

- ☐ a. describing Rimbaud's poetry.
- ☐ b. comparing Rimbaud to Verlaine.
- ☐ c. recalling other people's descriptions of Rimbaud.
- ☐ d. telling facts about Rimbaud's life.

_____

Vocabulary in Context

6 As used in this passage, a _focus_ is

- ☐ a. a point of attraction.
- ☐ b. one of the points in an ellipse.
- ☐ c. the spot where everything is clear.
- ☐ d. the starting place of an earthquake.

_____

Add your scores for questions 1-6. Enter the total here and on the graph on page 239.

Total Score ☐

Answer Key

Passage 1:	1a. M	1b. B	1c. N	2. b	3. c	4. c	5. b	6. a
Passage 2:	1a. M	1b. B	1c. N	2. c	3. d	4. b	5. a	6. c
Passage 3:	1a. M	1b. B	1c. N	2. b	3. d	4. a	5. c	6. c
Passage 4:	1a. M	1b. B	1c. N	2. c	3. d	4. b	5. a	6. b
Passage 5:	1a. M	1b. N	1c. B	2. c	3. b	4. c	5. b	6. b
Passage 6:	1a. N	1b. B	1c. M	2. c	3. c	4. d	5. a	6. b
Passage 7:	1a. M	1b. N	1c. B	2. a	3. c	4. d	5. b	6. c
Passage 8:	1a. B	1b. M	1c. N	2. a	3. b	4. c	5. d	6. b
Passage 9:	1a. B	1b. M	1c. N	2. c	3. d	4. b	5. c	6. a
Passage 10:	1a. M	1b. N	1c. B	2. c	3. c	4. d	5. b	6. c
Passage 11:	1a. N	1b. M	1c. B	2. c	3. c	4. c	5. b	6. c
Passage 12:	1a. N	1b. B	1c. M	2. c	3. b	4. c	5. b	6. a
Passage 13:	1a. M	1b. B	1c. N	2. b	3. d	4. a	5. c	6. c
Passage 14:	1a. N	1b. B	1c. M	2. a	3. b	4. d	5. a	6. a
Passage 15:	1a. N	1b. B	1c. M	2. c	3. d	4. a	5. d	6. d
Passage 16:	1a. N	1b. M	1c. B	2. b	3. c	4. d	5. a	6. b
Passage 17:	1a. M	1b. N	1c. B	2. c	3. d	4. b	5. a	6. b
Passage 18:	1a. M	1b. N	1c. B	2. b	3. c	4. c	5. d	6. b
Passage 19:	1a. M	1b. N	1c. B	2. b	3. b	4. a	5. d	6. c
Passage 20:	1a. N	1b. M	1c. B	2. b	3. d	4. c	5. d	6. a

Passage 21:   1a. **N**   1b. **B**   1c. **M**   2. **c**   3. **b**   4. **c**   5. **d**   6. **a**

Passage 22:   1a. **M**   1b. **B**   1c. **N**   2. **d**   3. **d**   4. **c**   5. **c**   6. **a**

Passage 23:   1a. **M**   1b. **B**   1c. **N**   2. **d**   3. **d**   4. **b**   5. **c**   6. **c**

Passage 24:   1a. **N**   1b. **M**   1c. **B**   2. **c**   3. **d**   4. **a**   5. **d**   6. **c**

Passage 25:   1a. **B**   1b. **N**   1c. **M**   2. **b**   3. **a**   4. **b**   5. **c**   6. **a**

Passage 26:   1a. **B**   1b. **N**   1c. **M**   2. **b**   3. **d**   4. **b**   5. **b**   6. **a**

Passage 27:   1a. **M**   1b. **B**   1c. **N**   2. **c**   3. **b**   4. **c**   5. **a**   6. **c**

Passage 28:   1a. **M**   1b. **B**   1c. **N**   2. **d**   3. **b**   4. **b**   5. **d**   6. **b**

Passage 29:   1a. **M**   1b. **N**   1c. **B**   2. **b**   3. **c**   4. **a**   5. **b**   6. **c**

Passage 30:   1a. **M**   1b. **N**   1c. **B**   2. **c**   3. **d**   4. **b**   5. **c**   6. **a**

Passage 31:   1a. **M**   1b. **N**   1c. **B**   2. **c**   3. **c**   4. **d**   5. **b**   6. **a**

Passage 32:   1a. **B**   1b. **M**   1c. **N**   2. **b**   3. **c**   4. **b**   5. **d**   6. **a**

Passage 33:   1a. **B**   1b. **N**   1c. **M**   2. **c**   3. **c**   4. **c**   5. **c**   6. **c**

Passage 34:   1a. **B**   1b. **M**   1c. **N**   2. **b**   3. **d**   4. **a**   5. **c**   6. **b**

Passage 35:   1a. **B**   1b. **N**   1c. **M**   2. **b**   3. **b**   4. **d**   5. **a**   6. **c**

Passage 36:   1a. **N**   1b. **B**   1c. **M**   2. **a**   3. **a**   4. **d**   5. **b**   6. **c**

Passage 37:   1a. **N**   1b. **M**   1c. **B**   2. **b**   3. **b**   4. **d**   5. **c**   6. **c**

Passage 38:   1a. **B**   1b. **N**   1c. **M**   2. **b**   3. **b**   4. **a**   5. **b**   6. **a**

Passage 39:   1a. **M**   1b. **B**   1c. **N**   2. **d**   3. **b**   4. **c**   5. **c**   6. **b**

Passage 40:   1a. **M**   1b. **N**   1c. **B**   2. **c**   3. **d**   4. **b**   5. **d**   6. **a**

Passage 41:	1a. **M**	1b. **B**	1c. **N**	2. c	3. a	4. c	5. c	6. c
Passage 42:	1a. **N**	1b. **M**	1c. **B**	2. b	3. d	4. b	5. a	6. c
Passage 43:	1a. **M**	1b. **B**	1c. **N**	2. d	3. a	4. c	5. b	6. b
Passage 44:	1a. **M**	1b. **N**	1c. **B**	2. c	3. c	4. b	5. d	6. b
Passage 45:	1a. **N**	1b. **B**	1c. **M**	2. b	3. a	4. d	5. d	6. b
Passage 46:	1a. **M**	1b. **B**	1c. **N**	2. b	3. c	4. d	5. c	6. d
Passage 47:	1a. **N**	1b. **B**	1c. **M**	2. c	3. c	4. a	5. c	6. b
Passage 48:	1a. **B**	1b. **M**	1c. **N**	2. c	3. b	4. d	5. c	6. a
Passage 49:	1a. **M**	1b. **B**	1c. **N**	2. c	3. a	4. d	5. b	6. c
Passage 50:	1a. **M**	1b. **N**	1c. **B**	2. c	3. b	4. a	5. b	6. a
Passage 51:	1a. **N**	1b. **B**	1c. **M**	2. b	3. d	4. a	5. c	6. d
Passage 52:	1a. **B**	1b. **M**	1c. **N**	2. b	3. c	4. c	5. b	6. c
Passage 53:	1a. **B**	1b. **N**	1c. **M**	2. b	3. a	4. c	5. a	6. c
Passage 54:	1a. **N**	1b. **M**	1c. **B**	2. d	3. d	4. b	5. a	6. b
Passage 55:	1a. **M**	1b. **N**	1c. **B**	2. c	3. c	4. c	5. b	6. c
Passage 56:	1a. **M**	1b. **B**	1c. **N**	2. b	3. a	4. c	5. d	6. b
Passage 57:	1a. **N**	1b. **B**	1c. **M**	2. d	3. a	4. c	5. b	6. d
Passage 58:	1a. **B**	1b. **N**	1c. **M**	2. a	3. d	4. d	5. d	6. d
Passage 59:	1a. **M**	1b. **B**	1c. **N**	2. b	3. c	4. b	5. b	6. a
Passage 60:	1a. **M**	1b. **N**	1c. **B**	2. d	3. c	4. d	5. a	6. b

Passage 61:   1a. **N**   1b. **B**   1c. **M**   2. **b**   3. **d**   4. **c**   5. **c**   6. **b**

Passage 62:   1a. **N**   1b. **M**   1c. **B**   2. **b**   3. **d**   4. **c**   5. **b**   6. **c**

Passage 63:   1a. **B**   1b. **M**   1c. **N**   2. **c**   3. **d**   4. **b**   5. **b**   6. **a**

Passage 64:   1a. **B**   1b. **N**   1c. **M**   2. **d**   3. **c**   4. **b**   5. **a**   6. **d**

Passage 65:   1a. **M**   1b. **B**   1c. **N**   2. **a**   3. **d**   4. **b**   5. **c**   6. **b**

Passage 66:   1a. **M**   1b. **B**   1c. **N**   2. **c**   3. **d**   4. **c**   5. **c**   6. **d**

Passage 67:   1a. **M**   1b. **N**   1c. **B**   2. **c**   3. **b**   4. **d**   5. **c**   6. **b**

Passage 68:   1a. **B**   1b. **N**   1c. **M**   2. **c**   3. **b**   4. **b**   5. **a**   6. **b**

Passage 69:   1a. **N**   1b. **B**   1c. **M**   2. **d**   3. **a**   4. **c**   5. **b**   6. **c**

Passage 70:   1a. **N**   1b. **M**   1c. **B**   2. **b**   3. **d**   4. **c**   5. **a**   6. **a**

Passage 71:   1a. **M**   1b. **B**   1c. **N**   2. **c**   3. **c**   4. **a**   5. **b**   6. **b**

Passage 72:   1a. **B**   1b. **N**   1c. **M**   2. **c**   3. **d**   4. **b**   5. **d**   6. **c**

Passage 73:   1a. **M**   1b. **N**   1c. **B**   2. **c**   3. **c**   4. **b**   5. **c**   6. **c**

Passage 74:   1a. **M**   1b. **B**   1c. **N**   2. **c**   3. **b**   4. **a**   5. **b**   6. **d**

Passage 75:   1a. **M**   1b. **N**   1c. **B**   2. **c**   3. **b**   4. **c**   5. **d**   6. **c**

Passage 76:   1a. **N**   1b. **B**   1c. **M**   2. **c**   3. **b**   4. **d**   5. **b**   6. **b**

Passage 77:   1a. **M**   1b. **N**   1c. **B**   2. **d**   3. **d**   4. **d**   5. **c**   6. **c**

Passage 78:   1a. **M**   1b. **N**   1c. **B**   2. **d**   3. **b**   4. **a**   5. **c**   6. **d**

Passage 79:   1a. **B**   1b. **N**   1c. **M**   2. **b**   3. **b**   4. **c**   5. **a**   6. **c**

Passage 80:   1a. **M**   1b. **B**   1c. **N**   2. **c**   3. **d**   4. **d**   5. **b**   6. **a**

Passage 81:	1a. **M**	1b. **B**	1c. **N**	2. c	3. d	4. d	5. c	6. b
Passage 82:	1a. **B**	1b. **N**	1c. **M**	2. c	3. b	4. a	5. d	6. c
Passage 83:	1a. **M**	1b. **N**	1c. **B**	2. b	3. c	4. c	5. b	6. a
Passage 84:	1a. **B**	1b. **M**	1c. **N**	2. b	3. d	4. d	5. d	6. a
Passage 85:	1a. **M**	1b. **B**	1c. **N**	2. d	3. d	4. b	5. c	6. c
Passage 86:	1a. **M**	1b. **B**	1c. **N**	2. c	3. d	4. c	5. a	6. a
Passage 87:	1a. **M**	1b. **B**	1c. **N**	2. c	3. b	4. c	5. d	6. c
Passage 88:	1a. **M**	1b. **N**	1c. **B**	2. b	3. d	4. b	5. d	6. a
Passage 89:	1a. **M**	1b. **B**	1c. **N**	2. d	3. b	4. c	5. d	6. c
Passage 90:	1a. **M**	1b. **N**	1c. **B**	2. b	3. c	4. d	5. d	6. a
Passage 91:	1a. **B**	1b. **M**	1c. **N**	2. d	3. d	4. a	5. b	6. c
Passage 92:	1a. **M**	1b. **B**	1c. **N**	2. d	3. a	4. a	5. b	6. b
Passage 93:	1a. **M**	1b. **B**	1c. **N**	2. b	3. c	4. d	5. c	6. d
Passage 94:	1a. **M**	1b. **N**	1c. **B**	2. c	3. d	4. b	5. d	6. c
Passage 95:	1a. **N**	1b. **B**	1c. **M**	2. b	3. c	4. a	5. b	6. c
Passage 96:	1a. **M**	1b. **B**	1c. **N**	2. d	3. c	4. b	5. a	6. a
Passage 97:	1a. **B**	1b. **N**	1c. **M**	2. c	3. b	4. d	5. b	6. c
Passage 98:	1a. **M**	1b. **B**	1c. **N**	2. c	3. c	4. a	5. d	6. d
Passage 99:	1a. **M**	1b. **N**	1c. **B**	2. b	3. c	4. b	5. c	6. b
Passage 100:	1a. **N**	1b. **B**	1c. **M**	2. c	3. a	4. c	5. d	6. a

Diagnostic Chart (For Student Correction)

Directions: For each passage, write your answers to the *left* of the dotted line in the blocks for each skill category. Then correct your answers using the Answer Key on page 225. If your answer is correct, do not make any more marks in the block. If your answer is incorrect, write the letter of the correct answer to the *right* of the dotted line.

| | Categories of Comprehension Skills | | | | | | | | |
| | 1 Main Idea | | | 2 | 3 | 4 | 5 | 6 | |
	Statement a	Statement b	Statement c	Subject Matter	Supporting Details	Conclusion	Clarifying Devices	Vocabulary in Context	
Passage 1									
Passage 2									
Passage 3									
Passage 4									
Passage 5									
Passage 6									
Passage 7									
Passage 8									
Passage 9									
Passage 10									
Passage 11									
Passage 12									
Passage 13									
Passage 14									
Passage 15									
Passage 16									
Passage 17									
Passage 18									
Passage 19									
Passage 20									

Directions: For each passage, write your answers to the *left* of the dotted line in the blocks for each skill category. Then correct your answers using the Answer Key on page 226. If your answer is correct, do not make any more marks in the block. If your answer is incorrect, write the letter of the correct answer to the *right* of the dotted line.

	Categories of Comprehension Skills							
	1 Main Idea			2	3	4	5	6
	Statement a	Statement b	Statement c	Subject Matter	Supporting Details	Conclusion	Clarifying Devices	Vocabulary in Context
Passage 21								
Passage 22								
Passage 23								
Passage 24								
Passage 25								
Passage 26								
Passage 27								
Passage 28								
Passage 29								
Passage 30								
Passage 31								
Passage 32								
Passage 33								
Passage 34								
Passage 35								
Passage 36								
Passage 37								
Passage 38								
Passage 39								
Passage 40								

Directions: For each passage, write your answers to the *left* of the dotted line in the blocks for each skill category. Then correct your answers using the Answer Key on page 227. If your answer is correct, do not make any more marks in the block. If your answer is incorrect, write the letter of the correct answer to the *right* of the dotted line.

	Categories of Comprehension Skills								
	1 Main Idea			2	3	4	5	6	
	Statement a	Statement b	Statement c	Subject Matter	Supporting Details	Conclusion	Clarifying Devices	Vocabulary in Context	
Passage 41									
Passage 42									
Passage 43									
Passage 44									
Passage 45									
Passage 46									
Passage 47									
Passage 48									
Passage 49									
Passage 50									
Passage 51									
Passage 52									
Passage 53									
Passage 54									
Passage 55									
Passage 56									
Passage 57									
Passage 58									
Passage 59									
Passage 60									

Directions: For each passage, write your answers to the *left* of the dotted line in the blocks for each skill category. Then correct your answers using the Answer Key on page 228. If your answer is correct, do not make any more marks in the block. If your answer is incorrect, write the letter of the correct answer to the *right* of the dotted line.

	Categories of Comprehension Skills								
	1 Main Idea			Subject Matter	2 Supporting Details	3 Conclusion	4 Clarifying Devices	5 Vocabulary in Context	6
	Statement a	Statement b	Statement c						
Passage 61									
Passage 62									
Passage 63									
Passage 64									
Passage 65									
Passage 66									
Passage 67									
Passage 68									
Passage 69									
Passage 70									
Passage 71									
Passage 72									
Passage 73									
Passage 74									
Passage 75									
Passage 76									
Passage 77									
Passage 78									
Passage 79									
Passage 80									

Directions: For each passage, write your answers to the *left* of the dotted line in the blocks for each skill category. Then correct your answers using the Answer Key on page 229. If your answer is correct, do not make any more marks in the block. If your answer is incorrect, write the letter of the correct answer to the *right* of the dotted line.

| | *Categories of Comprehension Skills* | | | | | | | |
| | 1 Main Idea | | | 2 | 3 | 4 | 5 | 6 |
	Statement a	Statement b	Statement c	Subject Matter	Supporting Details	Conclusion	Clarifying Devices	Vocabulary in Context
Passage 81								
Passage 82								
Passage 83								
Passage 84								
Passage 85								
Passage 86								
Passage 87								
Passage 88								
Passage 89								
Passage 90								
Passage 91								
Passage 92								
Passage 93								
Passage 94								
Passage 95								
Passage 96								
Passage 97								
Passage 98								
Passage 99								
Passage 100								

Progress Graph

Directions: Write your Total Score for each passage in the comprehension score box under the number of the passage. Then plot your score on the graph itself by putting a small **x** on the line directly above the number of the passage, across from the score you got for that passage. As you mark your score for each passage, graph your progress by drawing a line to connect the **x**'s.

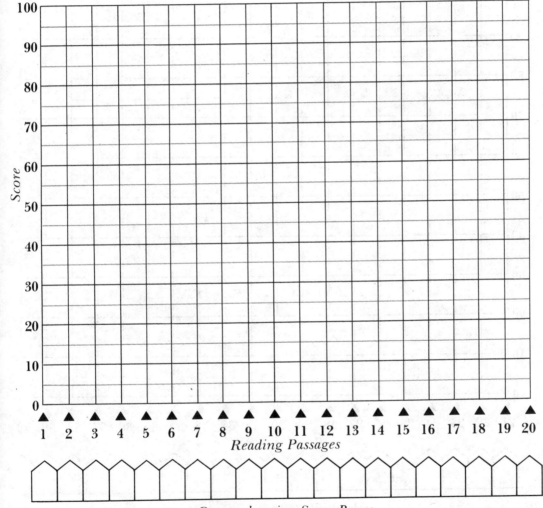

Reading Passages

Comprehension Score Boxes

Directions: Write your Total Score for each passage in the comprehension score box under the number of the passage. Then plot your score on the graph itself by putting a small **x** on the line directly above the number of the passage, across from the score you got for that passage. As you mark your score for each passage, graph your progress by drawing a line to connect the **x**'s.

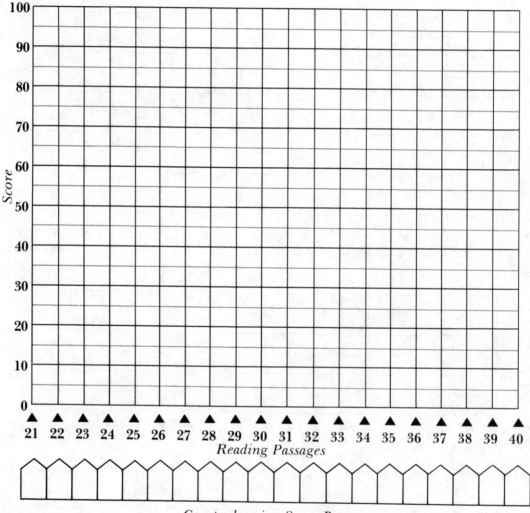

Comprehension Score Boxes

Directions: Write your Total Score for each passage in the comprehension score box under the number of the passage. Then plot your score on the graph itself by putting a small **x** on the line directly above the number of the passage, across from the score you got for that passage. As you mark your score for each passage, graph your progress by drawing a line to connect the **x**'s.

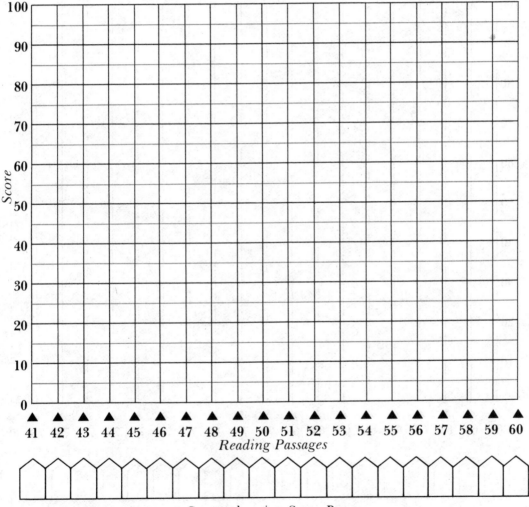

Comprehension Score Boxes

Directions: Write your Total Score for each passage in the comprehension score box under the number of the passage. Then plot your score on the graph itself by putting a small **x** on the line directly above the number of the passage, across from the score you got for that passage. As you mark your score for each passage, graph your progress by drawing a line to connect the **x**'s.

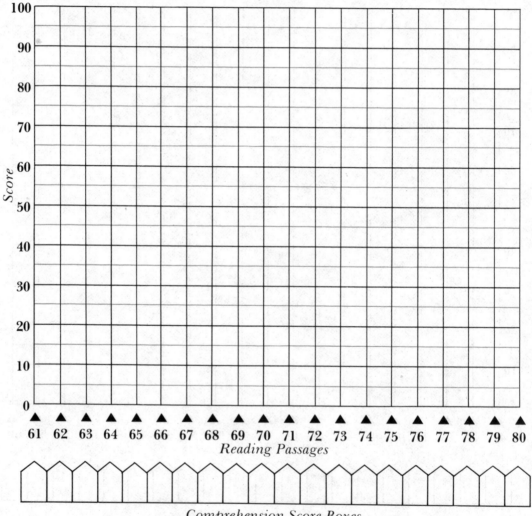

Comprehension Score Boxes

Directions: Write your Total Score for each passage in the comprehension score box under the number of the passage. Then plot your score on the graph itself by putting a small **x** on the line directly above the number of the passage, across from the score you got for that passage. As you mark your score for each passage, graph your progress by drawing a line to connect the **x**'s.

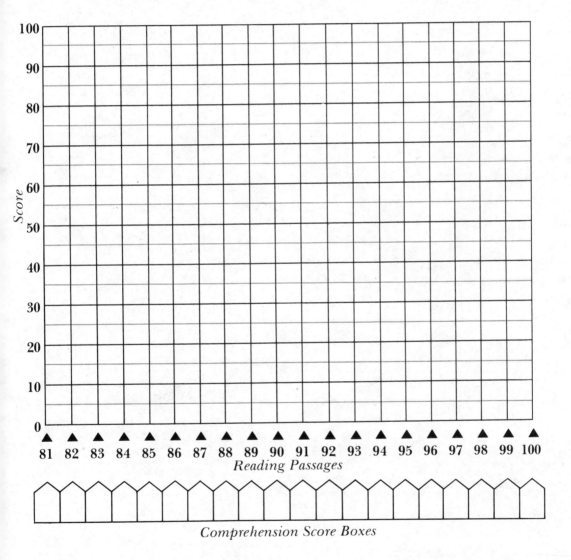

Reading Passages

Comprehension Score Boxes